Strengths Oriented Leadership

Strengths Oriented Leadership

The World Through Bee Glasses

Matt L. Beadle

BEP
BUSINESS EXPERT PRESS
Leader in applied, concise business books

First published in 2021 by
Business Expert Press, LLC
222 East 46th Street, New York, NY 10017
www.businessexpertpress.com

ISBN-13: 978-1-95253-818-6 (paperback)
ISBN-13: 978-1-95253-819-3 (e-book)

Business Expert Press Human Resource Management and Organizational Behavior Collection

Collection ISSN: 1946-5637 (print)
Collection ISSN: 1946-5645 (electronic)

Cover design: @whatneywhoston.
Interior design by S4Carlisle Publishing Services Private Ltd., Chennai, India

First edition: 2021

10 9 8 7 6 5 4 3 2 1

Printed in the United States of America.

Abstract

This book is about talent, strengths, and positive psychology. Everyone is naturally talented in certain areas and if we get the opportunity to use our talents at work and develop them into strengths, then we can work better, faster, and far more productively. Bees search for pollen, and they find it in the beautiful, successful, growing things around us: flowers. Flies search for rotting trash, bacteria, and ugliness. Do you want to go through life like a fly or like a bee? These pages present the overwhelming scientific evidence that strengths-based leadership and collaboration lead to more productivity, more innovation, better well-being at work, lower absenteeism, and better health. Learning to recognize your talents, leveraging them into strengths, and mitigate your weaknesses will leverage the way you and your colleagues work.

Keywords

talent; strengths; strengths-based leadership; strengths orientation; strengths-based approach; positive psychology; strengths-based teams; strengths mindset; intrinsic motivation; flipside of talents; prefrontal cortex; limbic system; reward mode; threat mode

Contents

Foreword

In this book, Matt Beadle shows what the talent activator can produce if you develop it into strength. *Activator*[1] is in the category *Executing* and is all about getting things done. I know Matt from our friendly, extraordinarily successful and joyful, long-term collaboration. Countless people, most of them managers from different industries, have given us feedback on how they have benefited from their new awareness of their talents and strengths both in their everyday work and in their private lives and how happy this makes them.

Matt has spent years practicing and applying what he has been preaching. Driven by his *Activator* and his *Positivity*, he is now passing this experience on to his readers together with his profound expertise. Thanks to his talent for *Intellection*, he has not only acquired an endless pool of experience and material on the subject of strength orientation, but also the need to pass this resource on to a broad audience in a way that is structured from practical experience and for practical use. He shares with experts and regular people alike the knowledge, experience, and joy of strengths orientation.

Matt lives life according to the principles of "doing" and "sharing" or according to the motto "good only happens when you make it." He has produced a book which starts with a brief reflection on positive psychology and the strengths-oriented use of talents, then leads on to constructive criticism and the use of assessments such as the CliftonStrengths and other tools. This book is totally geared toward practical use and contains authentic examples from both his own experiences and those of his workshop participants. This makes reading it as entertaining as it is informative. In his characteristically engaging manner, Matt captivates his readership with his wonderfully pragmatic writing style. You can see and empathize with his often tongue-in-cheek delivery of provocation, instructions, and anecdotes, which is sometimes half-joking and sometimes half-serious.

---

[1]All words in *italics* in the foreword are Gallup CliftonStrengths terminology.

If you happened to get out of bed on the wrong side this morning (with your fly glasses on), you might ask yourself why we need another book on this subject. Matt's extensive bibliographical index shows that he himself acknowledges that his book makes him just one of a long list of authors who have already examined the subject from multiple perspectives. If, however, you give the book a fair chance, you'll find that comparisons with other works are frankly irrelevant. The book doesn't claim to be a scientific study which researches and describes completely new knowledge. Matt's approach is similar to that of the CliftonStrengths publications. It is based on empirical observation and perception. The content of his 11-chapter work is based on countless real-world situations, questions from participants, and intensive intellectual exchange with colleagues. Its primary goals are to give interested readers broad access to the topic of strengths orientation, to share knowledge, and last but not least, to continue Matt's own learning process. This is the reason for the sincere request for additions and constructive feedback as well as feed-forward.

As a long-time colleague and friend, I respect Matt for his unswerving commitment to making his thoughts publicly available and for being willing to discuss them and to have them discussed. He doesn't just announce his book projects; he actually completes them diligently and with determination. In his workshops, he imparts knowledge and experience with both charm and absolute professionalism and manages to be both competent and entertaining at all times. My pleasure at working with Matt grows day by day. The discussions we shared during the creation of this book enriched and advanced us both.

I hope that all readers find refreshing insights for use in their everyday professional and private lives. Anyone who reads this book and deals with this topic will find that it delivers real added value in the context of their personal development and enrichment. Every journey starts with the first step and one step may lead to another and then another. Dear Matt, congratulations on this book and good luck with what is undoubtedly your calling.

Your friend and colleague

Dr. Martin Friedrich
Strengths Coach
February 2020

Note from the Author

What are you really, really good at?[2] Go on. Have a go, what pursuits do you find easy and deliver high performance in, almost without fail? Maybe you are a good speaker and don't get nervous when presenting in front of a group. Perhaps you have always found that you can quickly identify patterns in numbers or spreadsheets, even when the data are complex. Or have you received feedback over the years that you are able to remain calm in pressure situations and still come up with fresh, innovative ideas, even when others around you are panicking and fretting and wheeling out tired, old suggestions again and again?

What is interesting about this is that, when asked what they are really great at, most would probably respond with humility or even embarrassment at having to "boast," as they see it, about mundane, regular achievements. Indeed, most don't see such performance as achievement at all, rather as "normal, run-of-the-mill" endeavor. Many of us still carry with us powerful, lingering lessons from our childhood. "Don't show off, darling...be humble...it's not polite to talk about what you are good at..." our parents or guardians would tell us. Talking about yourself, your talents, and your achievements is often considered vulgar or self-absorbed and we are politely told that we should better turn down the self-aggrandizement dial a notch and focus on more important things like teamwork, strategy, and the bottom line.

Well, I'm calling bullshit on that, right here, right now, once and for all.

You are naturally talented at certain things and not only is recognizing and reflecting on those talents hugely efficacious with regard to your own personal development but finding the words to vocalize and share your strengths with others leads to a powerful culture of transparency where we each know and recognize each other's strengths and so work toward

---

[2]Interestingly, only about a third of us are able to confidently answer this question (High5.com).

implementing them more often. We will get to exactly what the difference is between a strength and a talent in depth later but suffice to say that reflecting on and talking about them is allowed. You are allowed to know what you are good at and you are allowed to share that info with your peers and process partners. What's more, I want to encourage you to prod and probe them for their talents too. If both you and they recognize your respective talents, just think what you might achieve together. This book is all about that. It is all about how good you and yours can be.

I have been a strengths mentor and leadership trainer and facilitator for over 12 years and I have coached over 18,000 executives, leaders and team members of diverse groups from over 40 nationalities, from organizations across myriad sectors in over 20 countries on,

how to employ a positive-oriented approach (aka "bee glasses," see Chapter 2),

how to recognize one's own talents and the talents of others (see Chapter 9),

how to leverage those talents into strengths to deliver best-in-class performance (Chapter 10),

how to intrinsically motivate others (Chapter 8) to get the best out of any given situation by employing positive psychology, and

how to build strengths-based teams (Chapter 11).

I have spent much of the last year on trains, planes, and in automobiles traveling around this beautiful rock of ours delivering workshops and talks on the subject of strengths orientation. I was in 19 countries for clients in 2019 and I must admit, the traveling was tiresome, but I used my time in airport lounges and hotel rooms to good effect. I have used it to put this book together. It is the amalgamation of all the material on the subject of strengths and positive psychology from my keynotes and seminars, and it has been a joy to write.

Every day is a school day. Enjoy the book, everyone.

Matt
February 2020

Acknowledgments

I would like to thank the following people, without whom this book would never have become a reality.

First and foremost to my editor Rob Zwettler, his colleagues Sheri Dean, Nigel Wyatt, and all at my publishers Business Expert Press. Having an idea for a book is one thing but that dream only becomes a reality with the help of such literary industry experts like you guys.

Professionally I have been inspired by and had the pleasure to work with so many incredible leadership facilitators and strengths coaches in my career. Many have contributed to this book, either directly or indirectly, and I say thank you to all of you. You are a credit to our profession. Christine Ait-Mokhtar, Doreen Köhler, Christiaan Lorenzen, Marion Schopen, Sarah Malone, Dr Philippa Ward, Lutz Pickhardt, Klaus Dürrbeck, Michael Knieling, Gabor Holch, David Liebnau, Dr Hans Werner Hagemann, Dr Paul Schürmann, Vivianne Naslund. A special thanks goes here to my friend, colleague, and strengths coach Dr. Martin Friedrich for so kindly providing his special foreword for this book and for all the chats we have had over the years about strengths orientation. Your calmness and Haltung has been an inspiration to me, Martin.

To my polyglot, linguist mother Bev for her tireless proofreading. Your attention to detail and talent with the English language never ceases to amaze me. You imbued all three of us with our love of words. Your mum would be as proud of you as I am grateful to you.

To all my thousands of workshop participants over the years: Thank you for the incredible questions, insights, anecdotes, reflections, and aha moments that I have been lucky enough to share with you. Facilitating and coaching so many people from so many countries in strengths orientation is a career I feel honored to have and I certainly would not have written this book had it not been for you.

To Achmed for calling me an amateur. To the guy who looked like Matthew McConaughey for showing me the way. To Mr. Travett for making me realize when I'm done. To Costas for helping me see about a girl.

To Glenn for having made me laugh almost every day this last year. Good man yourself. To CAM for taking care of all my travel debacles. To Uli Hartmann and Alexander Matthias for being brilliant educators and for their excellent contributions to this book. To the guy in the Arbeitsamt for introducing me to intrinsic motivation.

My brothers and sisters (both by blood and otherwise) Fred, Richard, Jack, Caz, Jane, Pete, Stu, Neil, Daniel, Etti, Marcel, Himmo, Johnny, Sadler, Marc, Eric, Normi, Raymo, Lainger, Jonah, John, Andy, Andy, Chrissi, Arron, Nils, Bear, and Momo. The balance you bring to my life gives me the energy to care so much about what I do.

My love and thanks go to my beautiful children. I am sorry that Daddy sometimes has to travel a lot for his work or has his head stuck in a laptop writing, when he is at home. I do everything I do for you and to hear you run down the stairs to greet me as I return home from work. I love you my prince and princess of Werther. Now that the book is finally finished, ice creams are on me.

And last but most importantly to my adoring wife. For the hours and hours of patient listening. For the ideas, critique, nudges, and support. For the decades of joy you have brought me and our family with your positivity. For being the most strengths-oriented person I have ever met.

For LSB

I've never met an effective leader who wasn't aware of his talents and working to sharpen them.

Former NATO Supreme Allied Commander, Wesley Clark

CHAPTER 1

Introduction

What This Book Is

They say—to really get your point across—that you should start, right from the get-go, with the main message (Minto 2009). So here it is, my key message:

If you want to achieve top performance, you have to use your strengths!

That's it. There's no more hocus-pocus here, no more (unnecessary) complexity. If you want to be very, very good at something, you have to start with talent. If you are interested in getting high performance out of yourself—or out of those around you—then read on. If you are happy achieving average, then this book is not for you. I'm not being deliberately provocative when I write that, I am merely being honest. It is simply a scientific fact. Identifying talent and implementing strengths can lead to best-in-class performance, period. Study, after study, after study[1] has shown us exactly that.

In this book, I'll show you the *overwhelming* body of evidence, which shows that we humans perform best when we work in areas where we can implement our talents and develop them to strengths (see Chapters 5, 9, and 10), when we work on tasks that challenge and stimulate us, when we work on things which we enjoy, and when we employ a positive attitude (Chapter 2).

However, despite the eye-watering amount of scientific proof from science (Chapter 7), from professional practice and from field study to the contrary, I still meet professionals from all walks of life—on a regular basis—who seem determined to convince me that strengths orientation is just wishy-washy, feel-good alakazam. To really get on in life, they tell me, we have to endure hardship, toil and graft on jobs that we hate, grind through our careers while regularly covering for our weaknesses, spend

---

[1] Don't worry, I'll point you in the direction of loads of these studies in the following pages.

lots of our energy identifying failure and underperformance and then even more energy, time, and money trying to iron out those deficiencies.

In fact, I hear such humbug so often over the years, that I have endeavored to address such critique directly throughout this book for those of you who may still harbor doubts about the efficacy of positive psychology and strengths orientation, even after you have finished reading this book.

Just to be clear, the message that I will present in these chapters is also *not* that success (in whatever form you understand the term) will somehow magically fall into your lap and that to reap this reward of a perfect existence, all you have to do is[2] *walk around with a happy smile on your face, notice the birds singing in the trees, thank colleagues for their help, motivate intrinsically, and work in ways that make it easy for you to utilize your strengths.*

Any author who promises you such a panacea is lying to you or mistaken or both. This book is not an easy win. It is not a self-help or self-coaching manual. It is not an instruction booklet to help you plug into some sort of *new you*. This is a presentation of, grounding in, and defense of two of the fundamental facts of human nature:

1. We can achieve more when we work[3] in a strengths-oriented manner.
2. Employing a positive mindset leads to better quality of life.

Let's crack on. We will start with a grounding in strengths orientation.

A Brief History

For hundreds of years, psychologists successfully developed a scientific canon based on "what is wrong" with afflicted patients with a view to then develop treatments and interventions to try to "cure" what is mentally, socially, or cognitively "damaged" and so bring them back up to "normal". Put another way, you identify (perceived) deficiency in people's psyche (compared to the norm). You then probe and investigate that "problem"

---

[2]Read the following words out loud with a light, high, wispy voice, while dancing round the room on your tiptoes and with your eyes looking to the heavens and your arms swinging gently above your head...

[3]When I write "work" here, I refer to any activity you engage in. It does not have to be of the paid, professional type.

before attempting to "solve" it. This mindset became the ethos behind medical systems we typically built up in the 18th, 19th, and 20th centuries in the western world and, largely, still operate to this day. These medical paradigms are typically referred to as "health systems," although one could argue that the process management and approach to treatment of deficiencies would more accurately deserve the title of "sickness system."

This focus on shortcomings can be seen across developmental, educational, and caring fields and has spilled over into the professional and public sectors. A mindset focusing on bottleneck-fixing and of "having problems" to solve had firmly dug its heels into society.

However, in the latter decades of the 20th century, different noises started coming out of the lecture theaters and laboratories of the psychological circles. According to Marcus Buckingham, three seismic contributions in particular contributed to the development of a new strengths-oriented movement, and all three started in the 1980s and 1990s.

1. The first took place in Cleveland. There was a medical center which purchased the hotel nearby to provide lodgings for its commuting staff. Unfortunately, the standard of the hotel was well below acceptable. The dining, accommodation, service, and housekeeping were all poor. Bad practices had compounded bad leadership from the management with low effort, motivation, and identification from the staff. The result was high guest complaint rates and low employee engagement scores. The hospital—wanting to solve the "problem"—did what many organizations do in similar situations; they employed the services of an expensive yet reputable consultant and charged him with the responsibility of turning the fortunes of the hotel around. How do most consultants start their work? They conduct a status quo analysis and that is exactly what happened to this hotel too. The consultant took stock of the current situation, interviewed staff and guests, observed processes, and drew his conclusions. He adjudged what was *wrong* with the hotel and implemented a rigorous new plan for the staff to follow. Sadly, the demotivated team didn't heed his advice and the hospitality provided by the hotel remained unacceptable. Undeterred, what did the hospital do, after the consultant's weakness-oriented approach was not auspicious? That's right. They employed the services of *another* such consultant. That advisor duly

conducted a needs analysis and surmised (in remarkable similarity to his predecessor) what was deficient about the hotel and its processes and consequently devised a plan (also similar) to improve the problems. Unfortunately their suggestions were also not implemented by the miserable team and the quality of the hotel remained low.

After the second unsuccessful consultancy, the hospital changed tack. In a new approach, they invited a then PhD student in organizational behavior David Cooperrider to take a look at their situation. Together with his mentor Dr. Suresh Srivastva, Cooperrider came at the "problem" from a completely different angle. He didn't aim his attention at the apparent negatives at the hotel, instead he asked the questions "what do we already have that *is* good" and "what would we like to become?" He interviewed the staff and helped them (re)discover what was positive about their place of work. Moreover, he took the complete team to shadow the employees at a hugely successful hotel. Energized and stimulated by what they had seen at the other resort and combined with their inquiries into what they already had that was positive, the team rebuilt the hotel into a very successful, quality establishment with satisfied guests and employees.

Regarded as one of the most groundbreaking contributions to organizational psychology, Cooperrider's theory of Appreciative Inquiry (AI) quickly became seminal. It developed into a simple four-step approach to help people and organizations better appreciate what they have that is already good and to develop a positive, developmental mindset to improve their lot and expand their possibilities. AI has become an influential catalyst toward a more strengths-oriented mindset.

2. The second game changer came from an equally unexpected source; namely a beach in the Yucatan. In 1997, Dr. Martin Seligman beat his nearest rival by over 3 votes to 1 to be elected president of the American Psychological Association (APA), a hitherto relatively conservative and cautious academic body involved in bringing together scientific and professional researchers and practitioners. Seligman wanted, though, to shake things up a bit in the world of psychology and move the APA from a traditional standpoint of examining ill-being to a new approach of working with researchers on *well*-being and on what that could mean for personal and organizational development.

To this end, he rented the psychedelically decorated holiday house previously owned by the Grateful Dead band near the Akumal beach in Mexico. He invited fellow psychologist and the godfather of *flow*[4] Mihaly Csikszentmihalyi and the two scientists spent the first week of 1998 with their families brainstorming and plotting what would become known as the theory of Positive Psychology. Seligman later mused: "we couldn't find a better name" (Seligman 2019). Good name or not, what they created on the beach in Mexico at the end of the last millennium was not just the label of a field of academic study, it became a movement and mindset which has since come to be applied across neuroscience, health, psychiatry, the humanities, and one which has even begun its march into business, politics, and society.

Seligman's main challenge was in upsetting the apple cart. The academic and professional world was firmly entrenched in the mindset of weakness orientation and treatment. "The old scientists and the old practitioners…" Seligman noted, "were sclerotic, overinvested in their way of doing things, and making their living from studying and treating misery" (Seligman 2019). Armed with investment from Gallup, The John Templeton Foundation, and most significantly from the Atlantic Philanthropies Foundation (funded from the fortune of Duty-Free magnate Chuck Feeny), Seligman set about building a network of young, as yet untenured researchers who would build this new academic area from the ground up.

Over the next years, Dr. Seligman was invited (and invited himself) to give a number of speeches including one seismic such talk, which he delivered for the United Nations. His words and the powerful message behind Positive Psychology were beginning to be heard by people in powerful positions and by the turn of the millennium, the word was spreading.

Consequently, Positive Psychology and its core tenet of promotion of well-being has become a genuine challenger and supplement to the widely accepted metric for measuring national success: gross domestic product (GDP), which was extensively used to compare the perceived success of nations throughout the 20th century. The problem is that GDP (basically calculating a country's total economic value) goes up when

---

[4]Flow is the state of contentment and ease we sometimes work ourselves into whereby everything seems to go right for us. The basket looks proverbially huge as it gobbles up the basketballs we throw at it. We find everything easy, fulfilling, and are totally immersed in our work.

people are unwell, depressed, sick, and even when they die. When sales of alcohol, cigarettes, and fatty foods go up, so does GDP. Funerals, cremations, medical operations, hospital costs, legal costs, etc. all increase GDP but are all a direct reflection of ill-being. Measuring a people's well-being alongside GDP leads to a paradigm shift in the political agenda and businesses across the world have slowly but surely started to follow suit.

3. The third is probably the best known and possibly the most influential of all. In 1988, Don Clifton's customer research and recruitment identification company Selection Research Inc. (SRI) merged with polling and market research giants Gallup. Over the next several years, Clifton, an educational psychologist, developed various assessment tools as part of his position at Gallup, to help companies identify the right talent to fill their positions. But the real quantum leap came in the 1990s when Gallup merged its resources and began developing an assessment which not only helped companies identify expertise but which, crucially, helped *individuals* determine what talents *they* had to offer. In 1999, the first 18,000 people took Gallup's new online assessment (more of this in Chapter 9), which was based on a modified ipsative scoring algorithm suggested by Harvard Psychology Professor Dr. Phil Stone. The test, which later became known as the Clifton StrengthsFinder® and is now called CliftonStrenths™ has since been taken by over 22,500,000 people including workers at over 90 percent of the Fortune 500 corporations.

The CliftonStrengths™ assessment's influence on Positive Psychology is not to be underestimated. It has become the most widely used strengths assessment tool across the world in companies, universities, schools, and professional coaching and has brought a late-20th century idea kicking and screaming into the hearts and minds of a 21st century generation of learners and thinkers. It has made an academic theory tangible and approachable and given practitioners the chance in many walks of life to identify their talents and implement them in a strengths-oriented manner.

Clifton dedicated his life's work to developing this incredible tool. He certainly left his mark on the development of this still young academic field and was rightly honored with a Presidential Commendation and named the Father of Strengths-Based Psychology shortly before he died in 2003.

One should waste as little effort as possible on improving areas of low competence. It takes far more energy to improve from incompetence to mediocrity than it takes to improve from first-rate performance to excellence.

Management Guru, Peter Drucker

CHAPTER 2

Strengths Orientation and Positive Psychology

After that little history lesson, it is time to take our first steps into the world of strengths orientation. And to do that, we have to start with the right mindset. Leading and working in a strengths-oriented way is impossible if you do not fundamentally concur with the philosophies that underpin the movement. It is not possible to *pretend* to implement a strengths-oriented approach nor is it helpful to anyone to be strengths oriented on Tuesday but switch it off again on Thursday. You cannot be a little bit pregnant and you cannot be a little bit strengths oriented. Before we learn the terminology; before we identify our talents and leverage them into strengths; before we even start *thinking* about building strengths-based teams, we have to accept the switch away from a weakness-oriented mindset. The tools and tips to help you and your process partners identify and develop your strengths are moot, if you do not start from a basic position of positivity. That position starts with how we instinctively perceive the actions around us.

The Power of Perception

Take a look at the equations in Figure 2.1. What do you notice?

Did you notice that one of the calculations is wrong? Was the first thing that your attention seemed drawn to, after having scanned across the image, that the third one was incorrect? Don't worry, if you did, then you performed in a similar manner to the vast majority of workshop participants that I have shown that image to over the last years. In Britain, Germany, France, South Africa, the Netherlands, Portugal, Romania, Spain, Sweden, and Estonia, the response is always the same. Russians, Australians, Japanese, Chinese, Americans, Poles—the response is the same. Thousands of

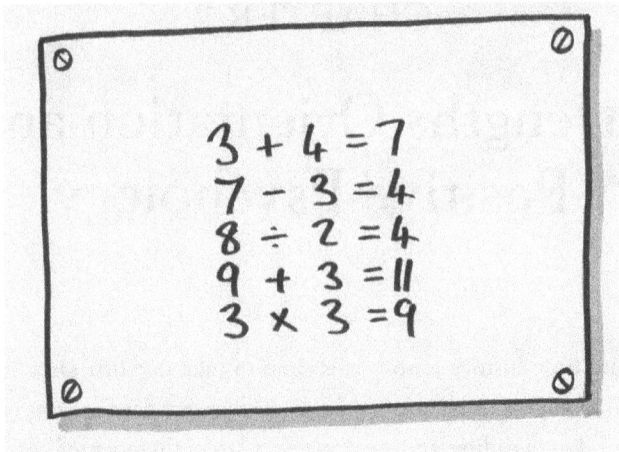

Figure 2.1 Back to school

delegates at my events; almost all, usually instantly yell out: "one is wrong!," shortly after having been shown that slide. Doctors, lawyers, business people, engineers, teachers, civil servants, factory workers, entrepreneurs, coaches, students, school pupils, designers, IT experts—they all notice almost immediately that whoever answered these maths questions got one of them wrong *before* they notice that five are right!

No matter who I show this to, almost all spot that one is wrong before they even remark (if at all) that five are right. In fact, when I ask people to look again and then suggest that five are right, I am usually greeted with a collective, nervous laugh. Most are ashamed that they spotted the hair before recognizing the soup.

The thing is, though, we seem to have developed the knack of spotting *the hair in the soup*, or the one small negative in a bowl full of potential. In other words; we are great at detecting weakness before we recognize strength. So many of us go about our professional or personal lives, all too often with a negative mindset and with our antennae finely tuned to notice the weaknesses and errors around us. We probably all know a boss, who pops their head up disappointedly from behind their cubicle the millisecond that we enter the office; a mere 90 seconds late. We have possibly worked with infuriating colleagues who pick holes in our work and highlight the petty spelling mistakes or grammatical slipups in our emails or reports. Many of us express our chagrin at the lack of free parking spaces near the store or lament the tardiness of the rail service.

Take the following example: There is an urban myth about this guy (let's call him Stuart) who realizes that he needs a certain tool for a DIY project at home. He surmises that he doesn't have a hammer and so quickly decides to borrow one from his neighbor. As his thoughts turn to his neighbor Neil and to how he will ask him if he might lend him his hammer for a short while, he recalls the last time he saw Neil. It was a couple of days ago and Stuart called out Neil's name across the street but Neil totally blanked him. Stuart then goes to his partner and asks: "Do you like our neighbor Neil?" but before waiting for an answer he simply piggybacks his own initial negative thoughts. "Forget it. That Neil is a right trouble-maker! He's not a nice guy at all. If I asked him to borrow his hammer, he'd probably refuse anyway. He's that kind of guy." Having talked himself into a rage, Stuart consequently struts into the garden and screams over the fence in the vague direction of Neil's house: "You can keep your stupid hammer—I don't want it from you anyway!"

In this example, Stuart allows his (incorrect) perception of a situation and his negative predisposition to stoke his initial (incorrect) negative instinct into a weakness-oriented and presumptive mindset. He sees everything through "fly glasses" and never once even tries on his "bee glasses" (more on these in the next section). His negative approach passes "what if" and takes him straight to the presumption that Neil had deliberately ignored him. Had he opened his mind to the possibility that Neil might have innocently not even noticed him that day on the street, then the rest of his downward spiral may not have even started turning. His negative, fly antennae are allowed to sharpen, though, when Stuart chooses again not to entertain a potentially positive alternative when he doesn't give his partner the chance to even contribute. Had he, then who knows, his partner may have helped him tint his glasses more toward the shade of bee with an argument or suggestion as pertaining to a positive aspect of Neil's personality. But his negativity-oriented mindset has firmly grabbed hold to the extent that he now doesn't even contemplate comparison or reflection. He's seeing everything and everyone through his fly glasses. Everything is shit and so he does what all good flies do; he smears himself in it and then spreads the shit around.

The shouting incident (the proverbial shit-throwing in this example) is probably the one that Stuart, his partner and Neil (if he heard it) will remember, yet it wasn't the driver in this scenario. It was the end game. How or whether we get to that end game is in our control.

We don't know whether Neil heard his awful, unnecessary outburst at the end or not but, had he, what might he have thought? "Why is he shouting at me? Why the insults? Who is he to talk to me like that? I'll show him…." And how did Stuart's partner engage with the whole unsightly incident? Have they joined Stuart in judging Neil through fly glasses or are they maybe angered by Stuart's outburst and ready to confront him with a similarly negative appraisal of his approach. Hopefully you can see how contagious fly glasses can be. Neil was Stuart's victim. Who might yet become Neil's? Now negatively charged, where might Stuart's partner spread the shit to next?

Sure, it is annoying when our train is delayed or when friends apparently ignore us, and no one loves a grammar pedant but is the fox worth the chase? Does our exertion of energy and emotion on these annoyances and weaknesses really help us (or our counterparts for that matter) in the long run? No it doesn't. A fly mindset can be awfully catching and it can easily gather speed like a snowball hurtling down a mountain. It picks up baggage left and right, gets bigger, faster, and more aimless as it rolls, and ultimately can hurt all in its path. No one is in control of a negative mindset. The mindset controls us. In fact, not only does it not help, it actively hinders us. As in the example with Stuart above, we can talk ourselves into all sorts of umbrage simply by listening to our inner weakness-oriented devil voice on our shoulder before we give a chance to hear out the strengths-oriented angel on the other shoulder. This weakness orientation (a cousin of the ill-being treatment we talked about in Chapter 1) has become our go-to standpoint, when solving problems or dealing with challenges. However, I would like to ask the question in this book that Don Clifton first posited over 60 years ago: What might the world be like if we noticed what is right instead of always focusing on what is wrong?

Bee Glasses versus Fly Glasses

Question: What do bees fly around searching for?

Answer: Pollen.[1]

That is right. Bees search indefatigably for pollen. And where do they find that delicious nectar that they crave so much? In flowers and

---

[1] It is surprising how many people answer "honey." But bees don't search for honey, they *make* honey.

plants. That is, they find what they are looking for in the colorful, grow-ing, developing, blooming, efflorescing beauty surrounding us. But they don't stop there. Once they have found their budding, flourish-ing booty, they instinctively and gladly swoop up and over to the next flower and spread the joy around. They literally find success and beauty and then proliferate it.

Question: *What do flies fly around searching for?*

Answer: … um…Shit.

Call a spade a spade. Let us be honest. Flies search for rotting, decay-ing filth. Decomposing trash is to a fly what a veranda light is to a moth. They seek it out, they can smell it and see it from a great distance out and, when found, they land triumphantly smack down in the middle of the shit. But they don't stop there. Once flies have found filthy, dying waste, they rub their limbs in it, smear it over their bodies, and then swiftly dart to the next stop and spread the crap around. They are literally shit-spreaders.

Last question for now: Do you want to be a bee or do you want to be a fly?

Would you prefer to *fly* through life spotting foulness and decay at all opportunities with razor-sharp instincts and then smearing yourself in shit before transmitting your collected funk to other unsuspecting flies nearby? Once you've found the shit and landed slap bang in the middle of it, smothered yourself and those around you in it, do you then want to take off toward the next unsuspecting victim to envelop him or her in your mire? Think of the ramifications and how many future flies you might encourage.

Or would life-fulfilling diversity, development, success, and achieve-ment interest you more? Would you rather have your antennae honed on talent and then use your wings and agility to help others grow and prosper?

Now, I know that the last couple of paragraphs run the risk of sound-ing cheesy or corny; like a message from an esoteric, spiritual self-help guidebook but the underlying message is hugely powerful and very rel-evant in both your professional and personal walks of life. Do you want to go through life wearing "fly glasses" or would you like to try on a pair of "bee glasses" and see how the world might look through them?[2]

My basic position and instinctive approach to what I see and how I perceive it will indubitably affect my actions and the reactions of those around me. If I go looking for the hair in the soup, you can bet your bottom dollar that I will find it. And this is where it gets interesting. If, while reading this you are screaming at the book "no one wants to eat hairy soup!," then do not fret. I am 100 percent with you on that. Not just regarding the soup, by the way. I am with you that weakness, error, or underperformance should be noticed. It should be noticed, acknowledged, and repaired. If the ceiling looks shaky and about to fall on a friend's head, we cannot just ignore it. "It seems that the ceiling will fall and hurt you, but I am employing a solely strengths-oriented approach and so I will turn my attention to that success over *there* and leave you to your ceiling-doom." Unacceptable. Fix the ceiling. Have the ceiling repaired. But, when you do, let two things be abundantly clear:

1. After you fix the ceiling you will have....*a fixed ceiling*! Nothing more. You will not, suddenly, be looking up at the ceiling of the Sistine chapel. Fixing weaknesses leads to: ... fixed weaknesses. It does not lead to best-in-class-performance.
2. While gawking at and duct-taping the busted ceiling, you were unable to achieve anything else. You could not use your talents and strengths to achieve excellence. You had no time. You were taping up plasterboard.

If we spend all of our time finding and fixing weakness, we will be left with a lot of *fixed weaknesses* and very little time for anything else. However, if you want to achieve high performance, you have to save your energies from wasted weakness fixing and engage your strengths to work on existing quality (more of this in Chapter 5). Furthermore, if you want

---

[2]It has, somewhat depressingly, been drawn to my attention that the bees, as a species, are currently in trouble. Yes, the bees' numbers are tragically dwindling but that is because of *us* and our pollution and our destruction of their habitat, certainly *not* because of their approach to life. In fact the metaphor goes further, because our bee genocide is, consequently, ironically hurting *us* and hundreds of other species in kind.

others around you to achieve their best potential, then reminding them of their problems and shortcomings only wastes their time (and yours), prevents them from investing energy in leveraging their talents, and passes the fly glasses on to them in turn. If you are always on your colleague's case about their deficiencies, then you will *not* motivate them toward accomplishment. You run the risk of creating permanent social rifts or even encouraging unethical behavior (see Chapter 8).

If you are a leader, which pair of glasses will you put on moments before entering the workplace? Will you instantly notice Natasha's somewhat untidy workstation, lament Grace's poor punctuality, or criticize the spelling mistakes in Paul's latest presentation? Or do you have a complimentary word for their performance in a recent project, a thank you for their help last week, or could you motivate them with responsibility for an exciting new proposal?

If you are an employee: fly glasses or bee glasses. Which is it to be? Are you going to let Sarah's annoying, squeaky voice bother you or are you going to take notice of their talents in organization and alignment. Are you going to waste pointless time reminding Janet that she shows no natural talent for precise spreadsheet work or have her spend more time out on the road, talking to customers. She always gets great feedback on her key account meetings. We will look at the need for strengths orientation in leadership in Chapter 11 but, for now, ask yourself: are you a bee or a fly?

Johnny's Report Card

Think back to the maths example at the beginning of this chapter. Let us say that it was not just an arbitrary example but that it was little Johnny's maths homework. Johnny doesn't have a particular problem with his maths teacher. He gets on with her fine and he would like to be better at maths but he just doesn't seem to have a natural talent for it. Maths tasks and equations, which his peers often seem to be able to solve relatively quickly, are difficult and exhausting for Johnny. He tries hard to improve his grade but he just can't seem to understand the concepts or adequately learn the methods behind the sums and equations. He is struggling in maths classes at school.

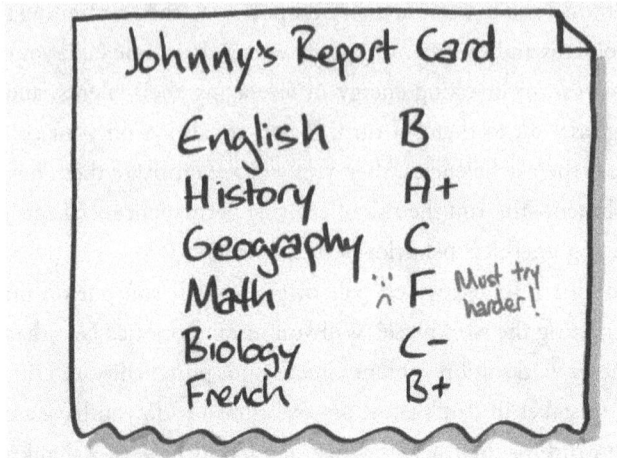

Figure 2.2 Johnny's report card

At the end of term, Johnny, like all the other children in school, is given his report card to take home to show his parents. This is Johnny's report card (Figure 2.2).

Please give a hand-on-heart, honest response to the next question: where would most parents or parental guardians cast their focus, if presented the above report card by their child? The maths grade, right? The vast majority (one study suggested that nearly 80 percent of parents would notice the poor grade first) would automatically turn their attention to the F in maths. Indeed, Johnny's teacher has not-so-kindly made it even easier for Johnny's parents to spot the F by adding a sad face and "must try harder" in unmistakable, unavoidable red ink.

Now that Johnny's parents have acknowledged the weakest of Johnny's performance this last term, where will they invest their energies next? Most will endeavor to support Johnny in improving his maths grade in time for the next report card. "Johnny, your grade in Maths is pretty poor. We are going to have to do something about that, aren't we?" Faced with such a dilemma, parents or guardians usually embrace one or more of the following strategies:

A) Arrange to speak to the teacher or even the head teacher to try to ascertain why the F in maths

B) Send the child to extracurricular maths classes.

C) Dangle the proverbial carrot. "If your maths grade improves in the next month, then we'll get you that new bike, you wanted." (see Chapter 8)

D) Sanction the child. "No more games console until your maths grade improves." (aka "the stick"—see Chapter 8)

E) Invest hard-earned money in online courses, apps, computer software, books, etc. to train Johnny's weakness in maths.

F) Spend time themselves, regularly sitting with Johnny to coach him with his maths homework.

In other words, most spend time, energy, and no little money focusing on Johnny's weaknesses. We as parents all too often create tension with our children by threatening to sanction them from their beloved pastimes ("the stick") or by offering to reward them for improved performance ("the carrot"). We sacrifice our own precious time to offer academic support in subjects we may ourselves not have excelled in and to which we have probably not given any thought for decades. We spend thousands on tutors, apps, gizmos, and gadgets and we encourage our children's educators to direct their scrutiny to our children's weaknesses in parent–teacher crisis meetings. For what? If we do all of the above, will Johnny's grade magically leap from an F to an A+? No. It will not.[3]

Might Johnny become the next Stephen Hawking or the next Steve Wozniak? No he almost certainly will not. We can flog that horse as much as we want but you cannot turn below-average performance into best-in-class performance unless you start with talent.

Looking at this from a different perspective, how many parents send their child to extracurricular geography classes, when handed such a report card? I.e. when the child shows excellence in a particular subject. The answer is very, very few.

It is interesting though: If children show aptitude or interest in *sporting* endeavors, then parents invariably reinforce that interest by signing their child up for karate classes or registering them in the local soccer

---

[3]Assuming the F is because Johnny shows no natural talent for arithmetic. The situation would be different, if his grade were the result of a social problem in maths class—communication problems with the teacher, for example.

team or whatever. Also, when little Kerry exhibits a flair for *music*, then we pay for a piano teacher to come round every Wednesday or we spend money on expensive musical instruments or we get her a place on the local choir. The same is true when little Andy demonstrates a gift for *dancing*. A call is quickly made to the local ballet school, dance shoes are purchased, and future weekends are spent in mirrored rehearsal studios watching Andy practice his first position. We parents and guardians often passionately support our children's talents in sporting or artistic fields, yet when it comes to cognitive ability we ruthlessly neglect it. In fact, we go one step further—we ignore strength and invest in weakness. The most paradoxical thing about this is that the vast majority of jobs in this society we have created, require cognitive strengths. A far greater number of students graduating from universities across the world this year will not enter into a career in the arts or professional sport. Most will enter into professional, technical, academic, military, social, political, service, or production roles which invariably require cognitive skill at their core.

I know full well about the world of extracurricular education. I went to after-school classes for maths every Wednesday for five years. Every seven days for two hundred and fifty weeks at that woman's house with two to three other kids, trudging through painful times tables and labeling angles with cos sin or tan. Half a decade of nerve-wracking, confidence-crushing parent–teacher meetings with maths teacher after maths teacher; one after another telling me to work harder and focus more in maths class. Sixty months of classes that my mother had to pay for—I never asked how much it all cost, but it must have been thousands. Five years of Wednesdays of my parents having to give up their time, driving me to and fro. 250 Wednesday afternoons when I could have been developing my talents in sport, music, or in the subjects I excelled in at school—in my case—history, languages, or social sciences. Lest we forget the CD ROMs I labored over or the special parent-homework-coaching sessions my mother sacrificed her time for. When I look back, I recall the countless times I argued with my parents about those extracurricular maths classes. I begged them to let me cancel the classes.

Mine is definitely not a criticism of parents who support their children in mitigating their weaknesses and I am eternally grateful to my mother for the energy, love, and money she and my father invested in helping me pass maths.[4] Mitigating weaknesses is important (more on this in Chapter 10) but what if we had spent even a fraction of the time, energy, and money we had invested in dragging me, cognitively kicking, and screaming up to acceptable standard in maths on leveraging or on developing my natural talents? What if I had attended extra language classes or extra history classes or extra social science classes on even *some* of those Wednesdays?

Furthermore, mine is absolutely not a criticism of parents who support their children's passion in sports, music, dancing, painting, or any other field for that matter. For what it is worth, I strongly believe team sports, individual sports, music, dancing, creative writing, sculpture, painting (and many other such pursuits) can offer children wonderful learning and self-development opportunities such as experience of group dynamic, social skills, discipline, self-expression, etc. irrespective of whether the child is talented in her hobby or not. Whether she goes on to become a medal-winning Olympian or top the bill at the Hollywood Bowl is neither here nor there such are the myriad developmental efficacies of hobbies. Send your children to clarinet classes. Sign them up for judo lessons. Buy them a pottery wheel to encourage their creativity. But please do so with the sober understanding that they will probably not become world renowned in that field.

However the question remains, if your child showed a talent for geography, for example, how might they develop, if you arranged for a geography student to come round and talk to them about their travels and research into earth science? How might your child react, if you bought them access to a huge online encyclopedia specializing in topography and geology or bought them a globe or an atlas? Where might their cognitive *journey* take them if you invited your child to explain to you all they know about tectonic plates? To explore that question further, I would like to shine a light on two very different school systems.

---

[4]I scraped through with the minimum pass requirement.

The fact is that given the challenges we face, education doesn't need to be reformed—it needs to be transformed. The key to this transformation is not to standardize education, but to personalize it, to build achievement on discovering the individual talents of each child, to put students in an environment where they want to learn and where they can naturally discover their true passions.

Education Evangelist, Sir Ken Robinson

CHAPTER 3

Development and Strengths

The Effect of Education and Parenting on Quashing Talent

A large body of literature has long since posited that strengths orientation and positive psychology should begin early in a child's life as a tenet of the official education system (e.g., White & Waters 2015; Seligman et al. 2009; Peterson 2006). To help you appreciate the important role schools have to play in developing the mindsets we carry around with us for years or even decades afterward, I will present a comparison of two schools I know rather well. Many roads lead to Rome, of course, and the following is not necessarily a presentation of the right way or the wrong way to educate children. There are myriad options for head teachers with regard to designing a learning environment for their pupils but I hope to show the powerful effect schools can have on instilling either strengths or weakness orientation in their student bodies.

When I was at school in the UK in the 1980s and 1990s, we sat in lines. We sat in lines on uncomfortable wooden chairs and we only spoke when we were spoken to. The classrooms had hard floors, long wooden workbenches or simple, framed desks and there was one seating option: "up straight." We never stood (unless banished to the corner by way of punishment[1]), and we were certainly never allowed to move, crouch, slouch, lean, or lie down. The teachers told us to "sit still" ad nauseam—excruciatingly tough for kids and teenagers practically bursting to fidget and bustle.

---

[1] In 1987, aged 10, I was summarily sent to the back of the class to reflect on some misdemeanor I had committed. In the warm room, I subsequently fainted, falling flat on my face and chipping several teeth in the process. My teeth are still broken today. Funny in hindsight but a pretty chastening experience at the time.

In my 11 years at elementary and high school, I cannot remember experiencing a single class having been delivered outside of the traditional classroom or lab. That scene from Dead Poets Society (Schulman et al. 1998), where Robin Williams' teacher character drags his students out to the quadrangle to have them march and clap to discern the stranglehold of peer pressure and societal norms was a scene confined to the cinema for us. Such an inspirational learning setting was foreign to us at our school.

The teachers preached from the front of the unair-conditioned rooms, illuminated by blindingly bright strip lighting, while we strained our necks upward to follow both their teachings and their scribbles. If we didn't understand something, we tentatively raised our hands to ask for clarity. If the mood was good, the teacher would repeat the point that he or she had just made and then move on without asking if the concept had been followed. However, if the teacher was not feeling in an obliging disposition, then questions would be taboo and deemed disturbing. We were seldom allowed to talk to each other in class. Another disturbance. Passing notes was also outlawed. In most lessons we had assigned seats, in which we sat for each and every class and the thought of swapping places either temporarily or for a longer period, frankly, never crossed our minds. I recall that I sat with my back to the window, in the same French language laboratory, every week for 5 years. I never once, physically, had the chance to look out of the window while learning the difference between my parfait from my passé simple.

Our Walkmans were to be strictly left at home and had no place in such a learning environment. There was no way for us to hear music or sound effects of any sort while at school, save for the hoot of the recorders in music lessons. Sticker swapping on the playground in the breaks was tolerated for a while and then banned together with all other ball and tag games on health and safety grounds while musical instruments were to be locked (literally) in the music room, only accessible after school had finished for the day. We were tested to the nines—it felt at times as though I sat more tests than classes—and our parents were then summoned to the school once per term to meet with the form tutor in a closed meeting whereby the sole focus of the discussion (the child) was the only party not invited to attend. We were sent home at regular intervals with report cards filled with examination results, effort grades, attendance statistics, and formulaic term evaluation texts, penned by our educators but, which often had the feel of having been cut and pasted from last year's report card with just the adjectives changed.

Matthew is a (insert adjective here) pupil, who concentrates (insert adjective here) when working (insert adjective here) in class.

We were given a small homework diary on our first day at senior school and were encouraged to keep it with us at all times. That little light-blue logbook was assigned a level of import akin to a religious tomb or an essential travel document. In it we were to record every homework task assigned to us, together with the hand-in date. When we submitted work on time, the teacher scored a line through the pertaining project in the book before handing it back to us to input the next homework assignment. I can recall with such vividness how much that little booklet weighed on my mind. If I didn't feed it with ticks to confirm homework completion, it seemed to grow and somehow occupy more space in my life and certainly more arena in my mind.

At the back of that almighty pamphlet was a copy of the weekly lessons timetable. Monday first period, Geography in room E-117. Wednesday 5th period, Modern History. Friday afternoon, Double Science with Mr. Oels. The schedule was to be followed, period. There was no negotiation, no flexibility, and certainly no possibility for us kids to suggest when we might best like to learn what. Our week would end, every Friday afternoon for 2 years, with Double Science, whether we liked it or not.

Aside from disciplinary showdowns in (head)teachers' offices (my stomach still turns over, all these decades later, when I recall the all-consuming fear I felt, waiting outside those rooms for some telling off or another. Such call-ups filled my thoughts for days and distracted me from my schoolwork terribly, and affected my mindset toward work and play for years) and regular school assemblies, where we were updated on logistical issues "the home economics block will be closed for renovation for the next week" or kept abreast of events "the prince of Wales will be opening our new gym in January."[2] I cannot recall one single sit-down meeting, where tutors or teachers discussed my personal development or my hopes with *me*. Not one single such meeting comes to mind. The careers advisor asked me what I wanted to become, after I left school, but no one ever asked me *how* I wanted to develop *while* at school. The

---

[2]He never came, despite the school purchasing 400 new chairs to proudly put out in the gym.

building was literally built for us students to learn in. The teachers were paid to craft curricula designed for us to develop and yet no one asked us, not once, how *we* would like to learn.

As grim and Dickensian as some of this may sound, mine is not an attack on the teachers of my formative years nor on educators of today for that matter. I would like to add that I look back on my school time largely with fondness and the funny thing is, before I became an educator myself (20 years after I left school) and began reading up on and reflecting on how we learn (known as didactics), I had not thought much about how we had been taught at school. It was all I had known. I had little frame of reference and, so I saw little harm in it. It seemed normal to me (see Chapter 4).

The problem was that the regimented didactic environment in which I attended school almost certainly stymied creativity, and was weakness oriented in that it focused relentlessly on failure (below average grades, missed deadlines, tardiness points,[3] etc.) and created a negative mindset that, agonizingly, stayed with me for nearly 20 years; way into my adult life. Success was rarely rewarded and the whole experience was utterly undemocratic. We the pupils had almost no say in our own personal and academic development.

Most of all and probably worst of all, the schoolhouse indoctrinated us into thinking that everyone should learn in the same way. No doubt, my teachers had their reasons for their rules. Presumably we were forced to sit up and be quiet and uniform for the purpose of order. A quiet, orderly group of students is, on the face of it, probably far easier to instruct than a chaotic rabble. But that is just the point: school (and any learning setting for that matter) should be designed for the students (and their individual needs), not for the teachers (and theirs).

The straight lines, crossed arms, silent classrooms, hard chairs, and little, light-blue homework diaries were clearly well intentioned but they hindered a glaring opportunity to allow each child to learn as he or she learns best. Put another way, we were treated as equal. *Equal.* A word that usually carries strong, positive connotations. Equality has been strived for and hard-earned in so many walks of like by so many oppressed minorities

---

[3] I got lots of these.

and is considered by most as one of the true inalienable rights. I wouldn't argue with that for one moment save for in matters of personal development. When learning, self-developing, and self-reflecting, *we must not be equal*. We must let people learn as *unequally* as possible.

Some young children in my town are positively exhilarated to hear stories about my school time. They sit open-mouthed and wide-eyed while repeatedly nagging me to regale them of my learning experience. It seems totally foreign to them and utterly fascinating that we were treated as average and schooled in such a weakness-oriented climate. The testing, report cards, rigid schedules, regimented seating arrangements, lack of transparency, and lack of democracy are intriguing to them and totally alien. Why? Because these children learn in a totally different environment.

Strengths-Oriented Education

There is a state-financed school in the small city of Bielefeld in the northwest of Germany called the Laborschule (LS; literally: laboratory school). The LS is situated on the same grounds as the University of Bielefeld and the Education Faculty of the University has strong academic ties to the school. Established in 1974 and based on the ideas of educational theorist Hartmut von Hentig, the LS is a so-called *labschool*, where the individual strengths of the pupils are put strongly in the forefront and the curriculum and learning environment permanently and situationally adjusted to suit the respective developmental needs of each student.

The 700 or so children who attend the LS from the grades of 0 to 10 learn in a unique setting and develop a mindset vastly different from the school adventure, I described above. Let us take a brief look at what they do differently.

There are no classrooms at the LS, only *Fläche* (areas). Each Fläche has three groups of about 20 to 23 kids, who can move freely throughout the day—not only across their own area but within the whole school building. If a pupil who would normally have her classes on Fläche 4 wants to listen to a story being read by the teacher on Fläche 2, she simply excuses herself and goes and joins that session. There are no internal doors blocking students or faculty from any area in the school building, other than for the toilets. Each group is guided (the word "teach" doesn't really apply at the LS for reasons that I will cover later) by anything from one to three adult educators at any one time. These include classically trained teachers, social workers, special education teachers, integration assistants, outdoor education specialists, and trainee teachers. Part of the thinking behind the diverse range of adults available to the students is that people learn in very different ways and the more influencers available, the greater the chance that each child will be able to develop a lasting, stimulating relationship with his or her educator(s).

Democracy is a keyword at the LS. The children are able to stand for regular election to represent their classes (at all age groups) in the school parliament, which is not a pseudo-political body but a genuine forum for children to make proposals directly to the academic council. The democratic approach can be seen at a more anecdotal level as well. Teachers and social workers regularly ask their pupils what they would like to learn that day, week, or term and even who should do the teaching. It is often the children themselves. In the younger grades there are few set subject classes; that is, there is no scheduled math class, English class, or geography class. Instead, each child can discuss and lay out his or her *Wochenplan* (weekly individual learning plan) together with the teacher. If Hanna feels that she needs to work more on her arithmetic, then she sets herself goals in that subject for that week. Meanwhile, Raj may be enjoying practicing joined-up handwriting and so will set himself the target of working on that more again this week.

During so-called "Lernzeit" (learning times), the pupils choose what they learn and how they learn. In other words, it is not uncommon for the teacher to wander through the class during Lernzeit while his various pupils are each, respectively, working on maths, history, art, a foreign language, spelling, syntax, natural science, or simply catching up on some reading—all at the same time. The beliefs behind this approach are twofold:

A) that students have different cognitive and academic strengths (even at an early age) and

B) that the well-being and intrinsic motivation of the child deserves to have an agency and so the children are encouraged to reflect on what they would like to work on and how.

Furthermore, a key didactic tool, particularly during Lernzeit, is that the groups are made up of mixed-age children (up until grade 6). The youngest groups consist of zero, first, and second graders. After a small graduation celebration, the children then move across to the other building where they join groups consisting of children in third, fourth, and fifth grades. The advantages of this approach are obvious, when one gets a chance to observe, as a fly-on-the-wall, the school in action—something I have done a number of times. During Lernzeit, the children help *each other*. The teacher flits from station to station and assists situationally but the older children (benefiting from 1 or 2 years of peer coaching themselves) *also* share their knowledge with their younger classmates. Tellingly, they communicate with each other as children do, in their own, special childlike manner. This helps the younger children to be able to follow concepts easier than if a grown-up might overcomplicate a topic with adult rhetoric. It also creates a strong bond of trust and respect between the pupils. The older pupils also profit here from the "learning-by-teaching-effect" (Cohen et al. 1982), which has been known by educationalists for many years to help both the learner and the tutor. In the learning-by-teaching-effect, the (peer)tutors have been shown to improve their own understanding of concepts after tutoring or teaching others. A recent study investigated why this might be the case. One hundred twenty-six students were given 10 minutes to learn the contents of a text about the mathematics behind the Doppler effect (a sound wave phenomenon best known as the perceived change in pitch of an ambulance siren as it speeds past you. Its sound appears to change from a "nee-nah" sound to a "nah-nee"). They were then split into four groups: one that had to deliver a 5-minute class (with neither notes nor preparation) on the subject, one that taught a session using pre-prepared teaching material, one that continued mental arithmetic tasks, and one that was invited to write out what they had learned (similar to how we often self-study or "cram" for an exam). The group that had the chance to deliver their own, free class on the subject fared the best out of all students in a surprise test on the subject, a week later. We learn ourselves, while we teach others. The LS kids don't only learn from their adult educators, they learn from each other.

The democracy precept continues at the LS in the form of *WGKs* (optional subjects). Unlike many schools, which may offer their students the chance to choose between some subjects, usually toward the end of the school time, to prepare for particular assessments, the children at the LS can choose between a large offering of WGKs (two per term) from the age of 6. Whether woodwork, a third language, music, bicycle proficiency, insects, happiness and friendship, current affairs, applied math, pottery, culture, gardening, dancing, extra gymnastics, or caring for chickens, all WGKs are entirely optional, chosen by the students themselves and unassessed.

This they have in common with all other subjects (chosen or compulsory) at the LS. There are no graded written or oral exams, no graded essays, no graded homework or grades of any kind until the ninth grade. The pupils do have to submit work but the form (e.g., poster, assignment, presentation, etc.), the hand-in timing, and to a large extent the content or subject of the work is up to the pupil in discussion with the teacher. Grades are not awarded but detailed feedback and feedforward is given from teachers and peers alike. It is not possible to fail a class nor a year and children never have to "resit" a year or even part of a year (as is commonplace in school systems in most countries; Vitztum 2013).[4] The focus is not on testing; the focus is on learning. The pressure of deadlines and fear of failure is foreign to the LS children. Some critics argue that young people should be prepared at school for the high-pressure environment of many workplaces but the LS's philosophy is different. "They will, doubtless, encounter time-bound demands in later life so we try and allow them to learn about themselves here, while they still have the chance," Uli Hartman, deputy-head teacher at the LS.

If you were to take a walk through the open halls of the LS, you would see children learning in all manner of positions and places. You would probably catch some sat, typically at desks, some lying in "snuggle corners," on beanbags or on their backs, gazing upward. Some will be sitting on the swing, directly outside the classroom, book in hand, and others will be leaning against a bookshelf or perched on a windowsill, possibly with mp3 player earbuds in with their favorite pop or relaxation music

---

[4]Indeed, at present only Norway and Iceland in Europe allow their children to progress to the next grade, with their peers, irrespective of academic performance (Vitzthum 2019).

playing or with huge hearing-protection headphones otherwise used by hunters to block out loud gun sounds. The LS has learned that children learn in different ways. Some need the silence offered by earmuffs, some can work better with music playing in the background, and some gain benefits from standing, sitting, or slouching.

On a recent shadowing visit to a 0-2nd grade group at the LS, I observed as a group of kids found an injured bird during one of the breaks. The children handled the bird with care but wanted to know everything about it, its condition, and its prognosis for survival. The children asked their teacher question after question: "how long will she survive?," "can we put its wings in a splint, like I had when I broke my arm?," "Do birds feel pain?," etc. Noticing the fascination of her children, the teacher spontaneously threw out her lesson plan for the rest of the day and spent the remaining time helping the children understand the situation surrounding the bird. The genius in this educational approach was that the bird (organically) became the focus of the class—not the teacher.

What is funny is that when I returned home, I was initially critical of the bird session I had seen. I complained to my wife that I had witnessed laziness from the teacher. "She seemed to use the bird's plight as a way of getting out of usual classroom teaching for a couple of hours," I told my wife. But, after some reflection, I realized that my first appraisal of what I had seen had been all wrong. The teacher had expertly and situationally used the episode to advance the children's learning. The students were intrinsically stimulated and interested and so drove their own learning without need for any sort of autocratic, top-down direction from the teacher. The kids were in flow (see Chapter 11), they were working in prefrontal cortex (PFC; see Chapter 6), they were in a learning environment (milling about; outside) which seemed to fit the subject matter and made their learning experience a comfortable one, and their personal development exploded for those hours.

Alexander Matthias, a teacher at the LS for over 20 years, sums it up excellently:

> Education at the Laborschule is democratic. The pupils are encouraged to be involved in their education. It is their development and so we try to include them it as much as possible.

Again, my intention here is not to talk up one particular education system nor put another down. There are pros and cons in different scholastic approaches, of that there is no question. But the effect that any particular schooling policy has on the development of its pupils' ethos is undeniable. Hopefully it is clear that the comparison between my school's approach and that of the LS would leave vastly differing, lingering effects on their graduates.

Your attitude to work and leadership would be considerably different had you been developed in your school years in such a *weakness-oriented system* that led you to believe that:

- enforcing a particular (working) environment on your followers is your decision alone and their wishes should not be asked;
- every one learns, develops, and delivers peak performance in the same way;
- followers can only learn from their leader and the leader should be all-knowing;
- choice and democracy at work should be kept to a minimum to maintain order;
- pressure of deadlines, milestones, reports and other key performance indicators (KPIs) lead to increased performance.

Compared to if you had been educated in a *strengths-oriented system* similar to the LS and so assimilated basic philosophies of positive psychology, such as that:

- people develop and excel in environments in which they feel comfortable;
- average does not exist and delegates have different natural talents, which help them reach peak performance in countless ways;
- teams learn from each other and drive each other forward. Good teams attract talent toward them. Leaders are there to guide and support, not tell;
- ownership of decisions and processes breeds a culture of intrinsic motivation and fosters a high-performance mindset;
- stress, limits, and targets only blinker focus on (usually numerical) goals and extinguish creative thought and endeavors toward excellence.

If you were indoctrinated with a certain strengths- or weakness-oriented mindset or basic philosophy in early, formative years from schooling or parental upbringing (either deliberately or unintentionally), then that basic position could stay with you for years and, without asserted intervention, become your normal.

If your instinctive reaction is toward weakness orientation, your focus toward the identification of failure, or if you often find yourself thinking of the glass as half-empty or of a challenge as unattainable, then have a think back to your school days. Did they prepare you to fail, remind you of your weaknesses, and assume you were one of many or were there opportunities for you to identify your strengths and develop yourself individually in a motivating environment? If the former, what are you going to do about it?

However, it is not only our childhood experiences, which meld our minds. A great deal of our instincts was honed in us millennia before we were born.

We all live under the same sky, but we don't all have the same horizon.

Former German Chancellor, Konrad Adenauer

CHAPTER 4

2.6 Million Years of Training

Physical and Cognitive Strengths

If you and all of your friends and family had been alive 40,000 years ago, your lives and responsibilities would have been very different. The things that we class as important today; our boss' mood, whether the wrong kind of leaves will delay our trains, if we'll make it back from the shops in time for tae bo classes, how well we have separated our rubbish for the recyclers, or if the muesli we ordered as part of our online shop is family sized or bite sized were irrelevant and pointless back in the times of hunting and scavenging for food in tribes. Our forefather's and foremother's needs were simpler (Harari 2014):

Find or catch enough food to survive.

Protect ourselves from attacks from predators and other tribes.

Keep warm and dry enough to live another day.

Back then, the tribe members would doubtless have employed a simple but effective form of delegation. The tasks would have been divided up among the people in the group. For a small number of tribespeople to have taken on responsibility for all the tasks would not have been feasible or logical. (I cannot pick fruits and catch deer at the same time while keeping the fire going. Neglecting both or either may well have, literally, been a matter of life or death for me and my people.) Some would have scavenged for vitamins in nuts and berries, some would have been sent out on the hunt for protein-rich prey, others would have been tasked with guarding the camp, while a few cared for the young, prepared meals, or carried out repairs to the campsite.

How would our ancestors have divided up their responsibilities? If one of our tribespeople (let's call him Steve) had grown to be the tallest of all his people, then he would probably have been served with the respon-sibility for picking fruit. Let's say Steve is 6 ft 2 in (1 m 88 cm).[1] He has a naturally occurring proclivity (height), which makes reaching for fruit easy for him. Sure, Sarah—his prehistoric 5 ft (1 m 52 cm) partner—could also pick fruit but she would simply not be as productive as Steve. She could reach the low-lying fruit but she would struggle to reach the higher produce because she simply doesn't have a natural predilection for reaching up high.

Sarah could climb on a rock to help but such a tactic would limit her to the trees with large boulders coincidentally lying next to them. She could build some sort of rudimentary ladder or stool but that would require resources (e.g., wood, rope, etc.), time, energy (something she must conserve at all costs), and no little construction skill—all not very conducive to productive fruit-picking—and markedly slower than Steve. She could jump (also a wasteful expenditure of valuable energy and only conditionally precise) or Sarah could ask Bob the caveman to give her a helping hand up or maybe she could climb on his back but, either way, she would require Bob to leave his duties in the camp, so halving the per-person effectiveness.

However, over the years Sarah and the tribespeople have noticed that she is an exceptionally fast runner. The fibers in her muscles and soft tissue in her legs twitch faster than those of others in her group. She is perfectly designed to serve her group as a hunter, chasing animals to catch for meals. But her eyes are not the best. She has trouble identifying objects of prey on the horizon. Her friend Kelly the cavewoman, on the other hand, has excellent eyesight and can spot animals moving at great distances. When the two of them go out to hunt, Kelly spots and Sarah chases. The whole group eats well that night. Meanwhile, back at the camp, their prehistoric friends Andrew and Fatima, with their soft hands, care for the children of the tribe.

Fatima, Andrew, Bob, Kelly, Steve, and Sarah should all spend their time being as productive as possible to ensure their survival and the suc-cess of their bevy. And, to be as productive as possible, they should all work in areas of responsibility which were felicitous to their skills and

---

[1] Tall for a prehistoric sapien, but you get the point.

talents. The tribe would never have dared send Sarah out to pick fruit or let the slow and cumbersome Andrew hunt for prey. There would simply not have been enough sustenance. They would not have survived. In other words, the roles within the tribe would have been distributed according to its members' strengths. It would have been the obvious and logical step to take.

Thankfully most of us do not go day-to-day wondering where our next meal is coming from or whether our cave is going to be attacked by marauding raiders but we do deal with challenges every day of our lives, both professional and of a personal nature. The challenges have changed, but we should approach them in the same way as our forebears did all those millennia ago. We should situationally and systematically delegate tasks according to naturally occurring proclivities (talents). But we so often don't. We all too often assign tasks to those who neither enjoy nor exhibit a natural talent in them and yet we expect our people to excel in everything they do.

What is fascinating is that we notice talent when it is physical (height, speed, eyesight, etc.) and yet, when faced with the need to recognize cognitive talent (the requirement in the majority of professions today), we do not only *not* notice talent we actively *ignore* it. We insist that all of our staff are jacks- or jennifers-of-all trade and then we are disappointed and surprised when they don't deliver top performance.

This phenomenon is known as the jaggedness principle (Rose 2016). According to Todd Rose, just as a knife's edge is jagged to help it slice through bread or meat, so are we jagged, to be able to *slice* through life's myriad challenges. Moreover, that jaggedness is far from generic or routine—each of our blades is unique. As Rose puts it: "people have multiple dimensions and those dimensions don't really correlate with each other like we think" (cited in Cocoran 2017). In other words, just because someone has a particular trait, or proclivity, it doesn't mean they will necessarily exhibit another particular talent or predisposition.

Let's go back to our physical example from our cave friends for a moment. Steve was tall but his height was not a prerequisite for having broad shoulders nor does it mean that he necessarily be heavyset. Sarah had fast-twitch muscle fibers but not the best eyes. It is possible to be tall and light, short, and heavy or indeed tall and heavy or short and light. The one proclivity does not insist on the next's attendance. There are certain connections between the dimensions but there is not the correlation between different physical traits—that we may think there is.

And the same is true for cognitive and mental traits. Just because I show aptitude in mental arithmetic does not mean that my abilities to recognize patterns in complex spreadsheets will be equally propitious. You have the gift of the gab in one-on-one small-talk situations; you always seem to find the right turn of phrase, at the right time, to make your interlocutor laugh or agree or to keep the conversation ticking over nicely. But you don't feel confident presenting in front of large groups. Those words—which flow so freely over drinks before the event—aren't nearly as accommodating, when you're up on stage in front of that big audience. The teeth on your metaphoric cerebral blade are infinitely different and one does not preclude the other.

Think back to Steve, Sarah, Fatima, and the others for a moment and then transpose their strengths-oriented delegation to today's assignments. Do you, your superiors, or the people with whom you work delegate according to naturally occurring proclivities (like Steve and Sarah did) or are the tasks divided up according to some other, arbitrary (process-focused) system, which normally sounds something like this: "It is in your job description, so just get it done?" Sarah needed to exert valuable energy and time to build and climb a ladder to reach fruit easily grabbable by Steve. This seems immediately dim-witted to us: to have someone have to build something first to only achieve the same as someone not even on tip-toes and yet we set such expectations in our professional lives and with our process partners every day. We expect the colleague without a natural talent for self-organization to spend time and money on apps, stickers, folders, etc. to bring their structure up to only acceptable standard. "I don't care how you do it, just get organized. I want to see a clean desk at the end of every day." We roll our eyes when fellow meeting members can't instantaneously come up with a new, innovative idea in brainstorm sessions. "Why don't you contribute as many ideas as Oskar? Go away and come back with some fresh concepts for me by the end of the day." What might our friend achieve if he didn't have to spend large periods of his day struggling to keep his organization up to scratch with his boss' arbitrary perception of what organization should look like? What progressive work will be left to one side while she strains to come up with some new idea before close-of-play?

Different people are built differently and they identify, approach, and solve problems in different ways.

Sometimes there is even the assumption that because someone previously in the role did things a certain way, that you should/will also carry out your duties as such? "Anna always used to deliver a well-researched, pre-read document for me, before every presentation, so I expect the same from you." Just because Anna's talents helped her to work in such a way should not mean that her successor will have the same modus operandi. Many roads lead to Rome. What is more, our talents are the road map—not the road.[2] Whether we get to the church by crossing the bridge or walking through the forest is, based on our individual interpretation of the map, our decision and ours alone and, frankly, irrelevant. So long as we arrive at the church.

Additionally, do you or any of your colleagues sometimes assume type by thinking that because Hasan works in the accounts department that he will have razor-sharp mathematical skills, will prefer to work alone, will be very structured in his approach and a poor public speaker. If so, then you are doing Hasan and all of your partners, whom you stereotype like that, a huge disservice. Our talent sets are so *jagged* that the one does not preclude the other. Nor does one suggest the other. Hasan can be a numbers whizzkid *and*, at the same time, own the stage. He can be a powerful team player, yet prefer structure to out-of-the-box thinking. Hasan should not be thought of as an accountant. He should be thought of as a uniquely jagged individual, whose talents (each) deserve to be identified and applied.

The Unfairness of Fairness

There is a cartoon meme that has been doing the rounds on the Internet for some years now. It portrays a man, standing behind a lectern, addressing a group of animals. Attentively listening, he is observed by a small

---

[2] I am grateful to David Liebnau for this analogy.

audience of an elephant, a fish in a bowl, a seal, a bird, and a monkey. The man proclaims:

To make it fair, you all get the same task:...climb the tree!

Nonsense. That is not fair. That is far from fair. Indeed, that is *unfair* to the majority of the animals watching. The fish is thinking: "how am I to get out of this bowl in order to even contemplate climbing the tree? I have fins not hands." The seal flaps its flippers together in disgust, unable to grip the trunk of the tree. The elephant tries to climb the tree but ends up crushing it with one almighty step, while the bird soars above the branches, uninterested in such a seemingly pointless task like *climbing*. All this time the monkey, from his perch high in the tree (he has four limbs and a tail to clasp branches with, after all) looks back down at the others with contempt. The man, in his attempt to be fair to all of them, has been fair to almost none of them. He has set a task that only one is, physically speaking, ideally suited to complete. The bird and the elephant could *maybe* reach acceptable standard (after significant training or support) but their attempt at *climbing* would probably leave a lot to be desired.

When dealing with human beings, the phenomenon is the same. There is no such thing as fair. When we treat each other the same (e.g., by setting identical tasks or expecting identical results) we treat each other unfairly. It is not fair to ask carbon-copy completion from others because we complete in different manners. Just as the (physical) naturally occurring proclivity of the seal and fish make it impossible to complete the supposedly fair task assigned by the man behind the lectern, so are tasks assigned by leaders and managers the world over just as unfair, if they are set with the expectation of similar delivery. Expectations should be set so that performance can be delivered but our (cognitive) naturally occurring proclivities often do not allow it. Some people have natural talents in certain mental cerebral challenges but others simply do not. Fish do not have hands and some humans do not have a talent for reconstructing broken patterns. Monkeys cannot fly and some humans are psychologically unable to perform under pressure in front of an audience. Elephants can't clasp tree branches and some humans find it almost unnatural and awkward to show empathy and sense people's emotions or needs. I could go on all day, but I hope you get the point. Our age-old expectation of having our staff be jacks- or jennifers-of-all-trade (i.e., good at everything) is as fair (and useful) as asking a fish to climb a tree.

The issue here is that both the handless fish and the unempathetic worker have been *given* certain talents from birth. The so-called "nature versus nurture" debate, which has been raging for decades in academic and psychological circles (Ridley 2003), revolves around whether or not we are as we are because of the genetic code programmed into us before birth (i.e., given to us by our parents and foreparents) by *nature* or whether we in fact glean our personality traits, talents, interests, and foibles from those around us during our developmental years of *nurture*? It has been clear to us for hundreds of years that we inherit certain physical characteristics from our family. But the question as to whether we inherited mental and cognitive characteristics as well remained disputed. It is fun to think of social scientists and evolutionary biologists scrapping and rucking over their eternal disagreement, suede elbow padded jackets flying hither and thither, but the truth is that there is no need to settle it in the ring. There is now a clear winner.

Research techniques have become more sensitive and in particular with the arrival of magnetic resonance imaging technology in recent years, science has been able to come closer to an understanding of what constitutes our mental and cognitive makeup (Sternberg et al. 2016).

We inherit the majority of our personality and in particular our talents through our genes.

Probably the most conclusive of this work was the groundbreaking cognitive science research led by Professor Thomas Bouchard. Bouchard and his team closely followed monozygotic and dizygotic twins separated in early years and then reared apart in different environments and in different parental homes. The study followed 100 sets of twins for over 20 years, starting in 1979 and its findings were seismic in the nature versus nurture ring. Bouchard and his colleagues found that "virtually all … psychological traits are to a notable degree heritable" (Sternberg et al. 2016). Furthermore, "on multiple measures of personality and temperament, occupational and leisure-time interests, and social attitudes … twins reared apart are about as similar as twins reared together" (Bouchard et al. 1990). In other words, the upbringing the twins received in their respective separate childhood homes seems to have had only a minority effect on their development. That is not to say that kids' talent sets and personalities are predetermined at birth and that their parental care is of no influence to their development. But nurture does seem to play a subordinate role. Understanding that our talents are, to a large extent, innate in us is essential in developing a strengths-based mindset and it is only *fair*.

The Strength of Difference

After the Second World War, experts in the U.S. Air Force started noticing that the numbers of plane accidents were rising. Jet technology was in its infancy but proliferating quickly and the new, faster planes were becoming harder for the pilots to control. An investigation was launched to ascertain why so many pilots were losing their lives or narrowly escaping death in test flights. The initial assumption was that pilot error was to blame for the accidents but after investigation this proved not to be the case. Then the investigators turned their attention to the next logical cause for the accidents—the technology. Maybe the planes and their intricate machinery were failing. That though also proved, after investigation, not to be the case.

Stuck, the U.S. Air Force turned to a young physical anthropologist in their ranks Lt Gilbert S Daniels. Undeterred by the lack of traction in either of the Air Force's two previous approaches, Daniels looked at the problem from a different perspective. Maybe, he thought, the issue was neither with the pilots nor with the machinery but rather with how the two dovetail with one another. Maybe the pilots were not connecting with their machinery well enough. It turned out that the standard U.S. Air Force plane cockpit had been designed in 1922 and its dimensions were the same, 30 years later. The technology (i.e., the switches, levers, buttons, etc.) around the pilot had changed hugely in those 30 years but his distance to them and position in respect of them had not. Daniels theorized that the average 1950s pilot may not physically fit in the 1922-designed cockpit as well as he might. Maybe the body shape of the average 1950s pilot had changed, Daniels thought, making it more difficult for him to reach the relevant switches and knobs to save himself if the plane is going down. The assumption was made that if they redesigned the current cockpit to fit the average current pilot body size, then maybe accidents could be reduced.

To investigate his theory empirically, Daniels measured the body dimensions (e.g., height, girth, weight, arm length, leg length, hand size, etc.) of 4063 U.S. Air Force pilots. Using these body statistics, the Air Force then built a new standard cockpit for its planes, designed to exactly fit the size of the average U.S. pilot. What is your best guess? Of the 4,063 pilots whom they measured, how many of them had the same body dimensions of the newly calculated "average U.S. pilot?"

None of them did.

They designed a cockpit to fit the *average* pilot, hoping to help everybody and they ended up helping nobody. They would have been better off, had they taken the measurements of only *one* pilot and then designed the cockpit especially for him. At least then the planes would have fit *one* person. But they didn't even manage that. Their cockpit design worked for even fewer than one. It fit nobody. Why was this massively expensive and ultimately flawed research and engineering project undertaken? Because the scientists at the U.S. Air Force, with all best intentions, had made the all-too-common mistake of assuming that the concept of average exists within humans. It does not. Todd Rose sums it up best in his 2016 book:

> No one is average. Not you. Not your kids. Not your coworkers, or your students, or your spouse. This isn't empty encouragement or hollow sloganeering. This is a scientific fact with enormous practical consequences that you cannot afford to ignore.

We have been brilliantly designed by nature, thanks to 2.6 million years of human evolution (smithsonianmag.com), to be *jagged*, both physically and cognitively, in order to solve the myriad challenges that our environment throws at us. If we treat each other as average or expect average (or even similar) mental performance from those around us, we will only be disappointed. The person sitting next to you differs from you in well over 3 million genetic positions (Wayman 2012). None of us is average. There is no such thing as average in humans. We are all splendidly different from one another and to treat people as average and expect similar results from them is to do a disservice to their talents.

There is, however, a further cognitive can of worms for us to open. The 2.6 million years of development our species has gone through has left some other telling remnants behind beside our remarkable individuality.

Let people do what they want to do. You pay them (hopefully highly) for what they are doing. You have hand-picked them in an assessment process. You have picked the best of the best. Now you demand that they get signatures everywhere to justify what they are doing at the workplace. That doesn't fit.

Neuroscientist, Dr. Hans Werner Hagemann

CHAPTER 5

The Brain's Role in All of This

Cortisol versus Dopamine

It would be nice to think of our personality traits, emotions, and talents as esoteric, cabalistic superpowers, which we are magically and mysteriously gifted with by the miracle of evolution but unfortunately the truth is far more pretenseless. Like it or not, our character is not much more than the manifestation and result of a series of chemical reactions (de Groot et al. 2012).

The chemicals that are released by our brains are done so to help the brain communicate with itself. These neurotransmitters can be thought of as the messengers of the brain, whose job it is to leap from one of the trillion or so neurons in our brain to the next, carrying with them important messages of stimulation or inhibition (Beilock 2010). The neurons look something like an egg without the shell, dropped from a height with a splat on the floor. The tendrils of the splat reach out in all directions but, crucially, don't connect with neighboring neurons. There are billions of gaps between the tentacles of the neurons and it is these *synapses* which the neurotransmitters "leap" across to create our thoughts, feelings, memories, learnings, etc.

This seems odd at first. Logic would tell us that it would be easier to send messages around the brain with the neurons already connected like we send messages down a phone line but with the brain the opposite is true. We can only send phone messages in two directions along a landline telephone cable but the genius in our brain's design is that synaptic gaps between the neurons allow us to lay an infinite amount of telephone lines, almost instantaneously. The beauty of these disconnected neurons is that we don't always have to send messages along the same "cable". We can lay new synaptic pathways, i.e. we can learn new skills, information, and emotions, in the same way that a jogger can decide to leave the paved road and go cross-country, in any direction, through the fields. What is more, when the jogger treads the same route through the field again and again, then the way quickly becomes a path; almost as easy to follow as the asphalt pavement. Our brains work in the same way. That is, the more we send neurotransmitters along certain synaptic pathways, the stronger these pathways become for us. In other words, we old dogs can always learn new tricks. Neuroscientists call this neuroplasticity, which roughly means that the brain is malleable enough to subtely change its ways with concerted training.

Getting back to the messengers, these chemicals are classified into two general categories: neurotransmitters that stimulate our brain's activity called excitatory neurotransmitters and inhibitory neurotransmitters, which are used to send calming or inhibiting messages around the brain. It is the toing and froing of these neurotransmitters, which create our mood (upmc.com), but more on that later. Scientists are still discovering neurotransmitters as we speak but of the approximately 100 already identified, dopamine and noradrenaline are the most important for us when it comes to understanding our mental performance (Fabritius & Hagemann 2018).

Let us start with dopamine. One of the abovementioned excitatory neurotransmitters, it has become a sort of a rock star neurotransmitter. That is not to say that rock stars' brains pump more dopamine around than their fans', more that dopamine has become almost as famous and as talked about as some rock stars. It is referred to as the "fun drug" in thousands of YouTube videos and is discussed in terms of its relation to addiction, happiness, memory, and Parkinson's disease in countless magazines and daytime talk shows but the idea that its release gives us an on-the-spot feel-good buzz is slightly misleading. Contrary to popular opinion, dopamine (the neurotransmitter that hops across synapses while we learn) does not *itself* give us the feeling of happiness—but it is released when we are in reward state (Flagel et al. 2011). In other words, when we do something we enjoy, when we complete a task that gives us satisfaction, or when we deliver high performance, the brain *rewards* us by releasing dopamine (Fabritius & Hagemann 2018).

The other powerful excitatory neurotransmitter important for us when working with our talents is noradrenaline. Probably nearly as renowned as our rock star drug dopamine, noradrenaline is well known because of its connection with thrill-seeking, risk-taking types. Less a rock star; more a rock-climber. Those hoodie-wearing hedonists who leap from planes without a parachute or who climb skyscrapers without a safety rope are often affectionately referred to as (nor)adrenaline junkies. Ironically, these highly dangerous, modern escapist hobbies encourage the release of noradrenaline in a situation exactly opposite from nature's intended use for it. Noradrenaline was supposed to be used by the brain to heighten one's focus in life-threatening situations. It was intended to fuel our survival instinct by driving us to respond to perceived or real threats. However today, the free climbers and bungee jumpers *deliberately* put themselves into such challenging situations in order to release noradrenaline and dopamine to give themselves the kick of heightened focus. Although evolution designed them with noradrenaline to narrow their reaction on impending danger, they now self-stage that danger to feel the same charged state. What noradrenaline and dopamine certainly have in common, though, is that they are both directly connected to performance and arousal.

We will come back to both the fun drugs in a moment, but let us first turn our attention to their antithesis. We have covered the goodies; the Luke and Han neurotransmitters, but what of the Darth Vader of brain chemicals?

To meet probably the most evil of all the performance biochemicals, we briefly turn our attention from neurotransmitters to hormones, the difference between the two being that the former are released in the brain while the latter travel in the blood (Haselton 2018). Both, however, can be thought of as having similar roles, namely that of delivery agents for messages. The nastiest of all the hormones is undoubtedly cortisol.

The first problem with cortisol is that it only shows up when the chips are down. When we are stressed (either physically or mentally), the brain releases cortisol (Hormone Health Network 2018) through a chain reaction of a part of the brain called the hypothalamus, the pituitary gland, and the adrenal gland—known collectively as the HPA axis. The next problem is that, although its main roles are to help the body regulate important bodily functions including metabolism, memory, inflammation, and balance substances like water and salt, like most other responses from our ingenious brains, the release of cortisol is intended to be a good thing: bringing balance to the force like a sort of hormonal Jedi Knight. However (like a number of former Jedis), it sadly also has a very dark side. Chronic buildup of somatic cortisol has been connected to a veritable Galactic Empire of diseases and disorders including but by no means limited to: slowed wound healing (Ebrecht et al. 2004), increased chance of osteoporosis (Chyun et al. 1984), memory inhibition (de Quervain 1998), insulin counteraction leading to hyperglycemia (Brown & Brown 2003), reduction in the size and effectiveness of the hippocampus (a part of the brain) (McAuley et al. 2009), Cushing syndrome, mood swings, depression, and massive weight gain (hormone.org), proteolysis (the breakdown of proteins) and muscle wasting (Simmons et al. 1984), immune system weakening (Palacios & Sugawara 1982), and many more.

Cortisol is nasty. In fact, it is so nasty that it is the type of body chemical that would gate-crash a party it was not even invited to, then bum everyone out and ruin the atmosphere while it was there, and end up staying well beyond its welcome. Indeed, cortisol does just that. It is released into our system often unwanted or unneeded (stimulated by an ancient survival instinct still hardwired into us), poisons our thoughts and performance, and hangs around maltreating us much longer than we want or need it to.

So why the biochemistry lesson, you may ask. Well, to understand our strengths, we need to understand why the brain computes our decision-making as it does and how it steers our performance. For a more holistic treatise on the whole subject of the brain and performance, I strongly recommend you read the excellent "The Leading Brain" by Fabritius and Hagemann but in the meantime, here are its key messages.

Threat Mode

The last chapter was called "2.6 Million Years of Training" for a reason. We humans and our ancestors go back at least that long. Last year, I was invited to give a series of workshops in South Africa. On one of my free days, I took a ride up to the Gauteng province, about 50 km northwest of Johannesburg. The Sterkfontein Caves and the attached museum and visitors' center there offer a breathtaking opportunity to learn about the origins of our species. Sterkfontein was chosen as it was the discovery site of one of the most important archeological findings of all time; the oldest complete skull of one of our oldest ancestors, the species *Australopithecus africanus*. The skull, which has come to be known as Mrs. Ples,[1] was discovered by Dr. Robert Brown in 1947 and it dates back to around 2.6 million years.

After you visit the caves, you have the chance to wander through the museum's exhibitions. Possibly the most memorable of which lines the corridor of the ramp, which encircles the building like a leviathan bandage, leading down and down into the limestone rock. Presented on the wall of the ramp as it snakes down (it is the only way to get to the other museum exhibits) is a pictorial history of our world. It is very long and its key message is striking. In the grand scheme of things, we humans are insignificant footnotes on the mammoth story of this planet. As you continue along the spiral hallway, you pass dinosaur species after dinosaur species, age after age, tectonic shift after tectonic shift, extinction after extinction. On and on the timeline goes (it is tens of meters long) before we finally see the briefest of mentions of our species (and our predecessor species), which maybe takes up a few centimeters.

For well over 99 percent of the time, this rock has been spinning in space we were not even a glint in its eye. Even 2.6 million years ago when humanoid species started popping up on Earth, they bore little cognitive or anatomical resemblance to modern-day humans. It was only a few tens of thousands of years ago that we even started coming together into groups to lay the very first blocks in the foundations of what were to become the societies we have today (Harari 2014).

For hundreds of thousands of years, maybe millions, our ancestors roamed the lands as lone hunter-gatherers. Just another one of the many animals in the world all vying for their place in the circle of life. By no means the dominant world species humans are today. Their needs were

---

[1]Apparently Dr. Brown assumed the skull belonged to a woman because of its smaller size and so pronounced it a female: Mrs. Ples. However, some scientists today believe it to be the skull of a male *Australopithecus africanus* (durbanhistorymuseums.org.za).

simple and their actions even more primitive. They were imbued with the simplest yet most compelling of all instincts, *survival,* and had brains capable of cogitating little else—vastly inferior to the computing and reflective power of human brains today.

Think back to our cavepeople friends in the previous chapter. Their needs were only trifold: feed, procreate, and don't die. That was it. They spent around 2.6 million years doing little else. They had no need for advanced cognition to solve the nuanced complexities of modern life, nor did they have adequate brain anatomy even if they had wanted to. Consequently, those 2.6 million years of repeated self-preservation have trodden unmistakable synaptic paths into our brains, as strong as any concrete highway. Those paths are here to stay.

Whether we want to or not, our brains still instinctively prepare us *first* for survival and self-preservation before considering any other cognition. When we are faced with any sort of perceived danger, our brains resort to type and do what they have done best for a thousand millennia: they try to protect us. Although the complexity of our lives and challenges today are state-of-the-art, the background operating system we use to compute them is the same one Mrs. Ples used. We have since bolted on extra hard drives and RAM packs and installed loads of cutting-edge apps but our mainframe remains the same.

The brain's default setting is fear of danger and the ignition of self-defense mechanisms if that perceived danger materializes. Our forefathers and foremothers didn't have the safety provided by high fences, controlled breeding, ballistic weapons to protect them, or animal taming techniques. They were just one of millions of species battling for survival. Slower than most, rooted to the ground, awful swimmers, poor eyesight, worse smell than many, zero camouflage, and weaker than a whole host of larger, more powerful animals, humans had to do a lot of self-defense. That training made our brains pretty good at it.

Back then, when the saber-toothed tiger appeared on the horizon, the cave person's brain went into what neuroscientists today call "threat mode" (Fabritius & Hagemann 2018). A complete neuro-system designed for one purpose: survival. In threat mode, the limbic system (LS) takes over. The LS (the part of the brain found roughly in the middle) is made up of four key areas which can be remembered with the helpful mnemonic "a hippo wearing a HAT." The *hippo*campus is covered by a hat of the *H*ypothalamus, the *A*mygdala, and the *T*halamus.

As soon as we saw the saber-toothed tiger, the HPA axis in our hypothalamus released huge amounts of cortisol, which you will remember from previous pages, is primarily used to keep the body regulated but in such critical situations is used by the brain (together with noradrenaline) to send the message around the body that it is now or never. The messengers told the unneeded systems to shut down and heightened the alertness of the essential systems.

With their lives at danger, the cave people needed either energy and coordination in their muscles to *fight* the tiger, glucose in their limbs to run from it (*flight*) or complete physical control to hide from it (*freeze*) and hope it passes by. Cortisol and noradrenaline delivered those messages and the LS engaged threat mode. Energy was diverted to the relevant parts of the body with presently unneeded systems temporarily shut down or ignored.

This is why we sometimes get clammy or shaky hands when we are nervous (the blood rushing to the extremities; ready for action), butterflies in our stomach (the digestive system shutting down to preserve energy needed to fight or flee), racing heart rate (the heart hurriedly sending the goodies to frontline muscles and limbs), tunnel vision (we need to see the present danger clearly and cannot risk distraction), the need for fresh air (the body craving oxygen to power its fighting systems) and, crucially, concentration issues, muddled thoughts, and the inability to think in detail (the brain inhibiting potentially distracting reflective thought).

With threat mode switched on, the brain historically learned to defend the body against classic predators such as lions and bears but it interprets today's threats as just as grizzly. Whether the ball flies toward us and we instinctively put our hands up to cover our face or down to cover our privates—threat mode is on-call. By the same token, threat mode works in the same way when the brain senses less physical threats such as verbal abuse, workload pressure, bullying, discipline we judge as unfair, or a cognitive challenge we deem as too tricky. When our boss yells at us, the deadline nears, or the client remonstrates, we often feel our pulse pumping in our head, fiddle nervously with our hands, reach for chemical balance in alcohol, cigarettes, drugs, or calories, or just stand and stare.

Our ancient operating system identifies the supposed threat and switches on the *same* defense mechanisms. We ready ourselves to:

- Fight: "Hey. Why don't you just get lost, boss? Leave me alone!"
- Flee: "That's it. I can't work under this time pressure any more, I'm applying for a transfer to another department."
- Freeze: "Why didn't you say anything when the client complained?" "I dunno. I was lost for words."

But it gets worse. With cortisol flooding the system, there is one more, key issue. When we are in threat mode (i.e., working in LS), the part of the brain that could almost certainly solve our problems, sadly, switches off.

Reward Mode

Think back to the first questions I asked you, right at the beginning of this book. I asked what you love doing and what you feel comfortable and confident working on and most importantly on the times when you achieve high performance. It feels great, doesn't it? That feeling of satisfaction is the state the brain puts us in when it enters "reward mode."

Our ancestors had to learn to solve problems of their own in order to reach and ultimately remain at the top of the food chain. Because of their relatively poor physical attributes in contrast to the faster, stronger animals around them, their only chance of survival as a species was to beat their enemies mentally. They had to develop tools, shelters, and weapons to help them adjust to the—at times—daunting environment (we humans have been able to pitch our tent in the coldest north, in the wettest jungles, on the steepest hills, and in the driest deserts) and to conquer their animal adversaries. Every time that a sapiens (any of the anatomically modern humanoid species) invented a new tool or used her brain to outthink her prey or predator, then new synaptic pathways were laid down. As learned earlier, the more you tread those pathways, the more natural their actions become. Those successes would have led to prolonged survival, which in turn would have increased their chances of procreating and passing their genes onto the next generation. As these cognitive successes proliferated over millennia, the well-trodden synaptic paths very, very slowly began to be passed onto more and more offspring. The brains of our ancestors literally began to grow because of the talents and mental successes of their forebearers.

Today, our brains have developed so much that we have a complete brain part, which almost all other species don't benefit from. The prefrontal cortex (PFC) sits proudly in the front of our heads and appears (in smaller, simpler versions) in only dolphins and some monkey species. Built on the foundations of millions of years of good ideas, the PFC is the site of rational, creative, inspirational thinking capable by only us humans. What management trainers and startup owners call "out-of-the-box thinking," i.e., thought of the lateral, problem-solving kind all sparks to life in the PFC and the PFC's neurotransmitter of choice is the fun drug dopamine.

You may now be thinking, with this knowledge, that we are set. Easy. Do things I like. Set myself challenges. Work cognitively and the brain will drown me in dopamine happiness. I'll solve all the problems in front of me and all will be good. That is partly true but there is, sadly, a but. We *can* work in PFC and when we do, we are more productive and deliver higher dopamine-bathed cognitive performance *BUT* when our brain senses danger, the cortisol kicks in and switches on threat mode and when threat mode is on ... the PFC switches off! You read that right—our uniquely complex brains are only able to function in *either* of the two modes at a time. To preserve energy and after having swerved thousands of evolutionary chicanes, when the brain interprets an input as similar to something one of its pathways previously laid down as negative, then it has learned to shut down the PFC, inhibit the release of dopamine, flood the system with the hormone cortisol, and revert to survival instinct.

There is a monumental learning to take from this crash-course biochemistry lesson for professionals, students, academics, entrepreneurs, and anyone, frankly, who wants to work in "the zone."

We humans can *only* deliver high cognitive performance when we are in reward mode.

If a man is driving a car in bad weather and his car skids while going over a bridge, catapulting him and his vehicle into the icy river below, how might his inner voice sound?

> OK. So the car weighs a couple of tons, the bridge was 5 meters high, I was driving at 60 kmh so, taking the water resistance into account, we are probably sinking at a rate of … and the pressure of the water on the glass, which is 8 mm thick is.…

It, of course, would not sound anything like that. Probably more like:

GET OUT OF THE FUCKING CAR!!!!!

In such a situation, the PFC shuts off completely and survival instinct takes full control in threat mode. Admittedly an extreme example, but remember, our brain's old-school operating system does not differentiate well between the threat of a sinking car and the *perceived* "threat" of a job interview, the sight of a parking ticket under the windscreen wiper, the audience glaring back at us from our position on stage, or the lateness of a staff member. After the input enters the brain (e.g., you see or hear activity), it first goes to the receptors at the back of the brain before stopping at the LS. If the brain suspects it a threat, the pathways to the PFC are cut off and the action stays in the LS. Only if the brain deems it harmless does it even free up the signal to pass to the PFC.

I will say it again because it is so important: When we sense threat, our PFC switches off—vastly reducing our mental capacity.

There is one last hurdle with this whole neuro-odyssey (potentially the most hazardous hurdle): Cortisol (you may remember, I'm not a fan) stays in the system *nine times* longer than dopamine (I told you it was evil!). Furthermore, it is *many times* more potent with regard to changing a person's mood than dopamine. Put simply, we have a cognitive challenge on our hands to force our psyche out of its trained chemical negative bias toward the bad guys—cortisol and the LS—and into PFC. Our brain's natural chemical state is threat mode. It is frustrating but it has had 2.6 million years of practice to get into that damned routine. After 2.6 million years of constantly laying road surface, you would have a pretty solid highway.

Our job as executives and team members is to get people out of LS. We have a professional and, frankly, a moral responsibility to put people into PFC and get the dopamine juices flowing. We should be creating environments for our people, where they don't feel under pressure. They should feel comfortable, respected, and trusted. We should have people doing things that they enjoy and working in areas where they can leverage their strengths.

Amazingly, over the years when I have presented this argument, I have sometimes faced kickback. "The world cannot always be a cakewalk... life is tough, so we need to be too...you need to whip a horse to win the race... blah blah blah." I'm afraid to say, that such kickback is simply wrong and decades of scientific research have proved it.

It is not enough to be happy to have an excellent life. The point is to be happy while doing things that stretch our skills, that help us grow and fulfil our potential.

The godfather of positive psychology, Dr. Mihaly Csikszentmihalyi

CHAPTER 6

Strengths-Based Research

The Seminal Study

In 1955, the results of a study were published that shook the academic world to its core and began a body of research that, in the seven decades since, has conclusively shown that strengths orientation *just works.* The study in question was conducted by John William Glock and, as is so often the case in scholarly research, its intended focus of research was not the same as the earth-shattering results it ended up providing us with. Glock was an educational psychologist and in 1955 was interested in the relative value of different speed-reading teaching methods. He wanted, in collaboration with the Nebraska School Study Council, to see how three different teaching interventions would affect the speed at which the 10th graders in the experiment could read (Glock 1955).

It turned out that the different teaching methods showed no statistically significant difference from one another *but*, after trawling through the data, another incredible pattern emerged. It turns out that although the type of teaching method applied does not significantly improve people's potential reading speed, their initial starting point very much *does.* Glock noticed that there were two groups within the sample. One consisted of people who can read an average number of words per minute and the other contained those who seemed to have a natural gift for reading fast and could—without prior training—read significantly more than the average number of words per minute. Glock found that the average readers could read approximately 90 words per minute and that the gifted could read an incredible 350 words per minute with full comprehension.

Glock and his colleagues put both groups through their paces using various speed-reading training methods. Like I said, which training method was used didn't appear to make a difference but the subjects' existing talents certainly did. After the training, the average readers were able to increase their speed from 90 to around 150 words per minute. About a third of a page of single-spaced, typed A4 text. That is an improvement of about 66 percent. Excellent. Just think if your HR department sent you on a training course and you returned 66% better or faster or more productive or whatever. Everyone would be patting themselves on the back; congratulating themselves for a training intervention well implemented. The motto would be: training works. Right?

But then Glock had the above average readers (350 words per minute) benefit from the *same training methods* as the regular readers had taken part in. What happened was remarkable. After training, compared to the average readers who could then read 150 words per minute, the gifted group could read *2,900 words* per minute, with comprehension. Yes. You read that right. Two thousand nine hundred words per minute. That is an increase of over 880 percent. That is half a bachelor thesis—in 1 minute.

What Glock (totally unexpectedly) had uncovered was that humans can develop and improve their cognitive skills in many subjects but only to a certain degree. There is a ceiling. Unless, that is, you start with talent. If people show an obvious natural gift for something and one develops *them*, then the sky is the limit. Well, the ceiling can be a lot higher, in any case. If you want top, top performance, you *have to* start with talent.

So after reading about Glock's work, you may be saying something like: "That's all well and good, Matt, but who needs speed reading? We are professionals and we have completely different challenges." Sure. Ok, fine. So let us take a look at some other more work-related examples of research that shows the efficacy of strengths orientation.

Strengths at Work

Every year Gallup releases a worldwide report on the state of the global workplace, which they aptly call The State of the Global Workplace. They conduct nationally representative surveys in 155 countries annually, which cover 99 percent of the world's population. In 2017, they released their latest report, in which results from surveys from 2014, 2015, and

2016 were aggregated using data from over 31 million respondents. The numbers make for stupefying reading.

Only 33 percent of Americans are engaged at work. That figure drops to 15 percent when totaled worldwide and, amazingly, a mere 10 percent of western Europeans are engaged at work. But the Europeans are not the least engaged professionals. Only a pitiful 6 percent of East Asians are motivated at work. Considering that organizations in the top quartile (i.e., those where employee engagement is high) are 17 percent more productive on average and 21 percent more profitable than companies in the bottom quarter (Gallup 2017), we are witnessing a shameful waste of potential. Eighty-five percent of the world's working population is not engaged in their work, which is wasting a prodigious amount of potential productivity. Indeed, Harter (2017) suggests that this shortfall in engagement amounts to a loss to global business somewhere in the region of $7 trillion annually.

Just get your head around these figures for a moment. Averaged across the world, eight out of every 10 professionals do not get excited about going to work. They spend time at their place of employment just doing enough to not create waves or draw negative attention and so risk losing their jobs. Eighty-five percent of worldwide employees wallowing in threat mode (see Chapter 5), limiting innovation, ideation, and creativity. Eighty-five percent of the world's working population releasing cortisol into their bodies day after day after day—increasing the chances manifold of developing serious health problems connected to chronic somatic cortisol levels, which in turn puts health services worldwide under increased strain not to mention causing spikes in absenteeism (which costs companies billions annually). Eighty-five percent of the world not stimulated to go that extra mile to deliver high performance and so propel their team and organization to excellence. If just a few percent of us invested some time and energy into making the workplace a more comfortable environment for our people to work in, then many millions worldwide would be significantly and positively affected.

However, what is potentially more concerning is that 18 percent of workers go beyond disengaged and describe themselves as "*actively* disengaged" at their workplace. Actively disengaged sounds kooky but it is no joke. The old metaphor was the shop floor worker who literally "threw a spanner in the works" to stop the machine whirring to allow for a breather from the unmotivating work. Today actively disengaged might sound something like this to an executive at an automotive company:

Phone rings.

> *BMW Sales rep:* "Hello. Sandra here from BMW. How may I help you?"
> *Caller:* "Hello. I'd like to buy a high-quality car, please."
> *BMW Sales rep:* "Oh, you would like to buy a *HIGH*-quality car? Then call Audi!"

Hangs up.

Actively disengaged workers are currently sitting at their desks or working at their stations using paid time to plan and plot how they can best *mess up* their company's day. Leaders and team members simply must make more of an effort to mold engaging atmospheres at work. Creating an environment is just the first step, though. As mentioned in previous chapters, if you want best-in-class performance, you also have to focus on people's strengths. The trouble is that does not always seem to be happening. Leaders seem to be neglecting their employees' strengths and well-being.

Positive Psychology Studies

Back in 1979, around 12,000 people,[1] then aged between 14 and 22 years old, began what would become one of the largest longitudinal studies of its kind ever conducted. The study was called "How the Rich (and happy) Get Richer (and happier)" (Judge & Hurst 2008). I think you can probably see where this is going, just from the title, but humor me and read on. It is incredible. The 12,000 subjects, weighted for demographic, were interviewed in their homes, usually once per year, for the next 29 years on how satisfied they were with their job, how much they earned, what their current occupational status was, on their educational attainment, on any

---

[1]The original sample size was 12,686 but natural sample attrition has occurred over the nearly 30 years of the study.

health problems interfering with work they had, and crucially, on their "core self-evaluation." Core self-evaluation (CSE) can be translated here for our benefit as whether the subject lived their life with their bee or fly glasses on (see Chapter 2)—i.e., is the glass half full or half empty? None of them knew the purpose of the study and so couldn't second-guess its intentions. Its findings were astonishing.

According to Judge and Hurst (2008), people with a more positive attitude to themselves and to life benefited in so many ways in comparison to their fly-glasses-wearing counterparts: They were able to enter formal education earlier which seems to have helped them manage to snag their dream job more often and earlier in their lives. "People with negative core self-evaluations acquired education more slowly, which affected growth in pay, occupational status, and job satisfaction" (Judge & Hurst 2008). Speaking of occupational status—that was also higher in the bee-glasses group, as was their job satisfaction. Positive psychology leads to satisfaction at work. What a surprise.

People with a bottleneck-oriented mindset experienced far more health problems than those of a naturally positive disposition and those issues sadly fueled increases in absenteeism, which in turn negatively affects promotion chances, further education chances, and chances to earn more. You can see how it dominoes. Finally, and strikingly, happy people earn more money than those with a fly-glasses attitude to life. Indeed, people with a positive aspect on life do not only make more, they make much more; faster and younger. People with high CSE start making more money earlier in their lives and the speed at which their income rises accelerates as they get older. The high CSE group earned on average more than $12,000 p.a. more than the glass-is-half-empty group. Strengths orientation also makes you rich. Who knew? The happy group also pursued more additional formal education, opening up even further career doors. Strengths orientation just works.

Just to drive home the point, Judge and Hurst (2008) let us know how lastingly toxic a weakness-oriented mindset can be:

> Individuals high in neuroticism (a very negative mindset and low self-worth) tend to select themselves into more stressful situations, engage in more risky health behaviors, and have more accidents at

work, and they are more likely to be diagnosed with mental health disorders. Control beliefs [beliefs which may hinder performance] have been implicated in health behaviors in thousands of studies.

Bummer. Weakness orientation can be a real downer. But, once again, even more reason to accept that strengths orientation just works.

That is positive mindset, what about talent recognition? According to Matson and Robinson (2017), only 20 percent of Americans think that they use their talents at work. Once again—wastage bordering on the criminal. Such talent neglect is like leaving your all-singing, all-dancing, top of the range oven unused and cooking all your family meals on a camping stove instead or like leaving your sports car parked in the garage, while you hammer the jalopy down the highway; pedal to the metal. That means that 80 percent of employees are trotting off to work every day and not delivering the highest performance they can because they do not have the chance to leverage their strengths. Just imagine how much performance and progress employers are squandering. Think back to the earlier chapters in this book, where we talked about the importance of delegating and dividing responsibility in a strengths-oriented manner. If eight out of 10 of the people in your team are unable to regularly get into pre frontal cortex (PFC) in their job because they do not have a forum to take their talents for a spin, productivity will crash into a wall (the sports car would have nimbly swerved to avoid it). Workers who felt that they regularly have the chance to put their talents into action at work are far more productive and exhibited a more competitive edge than those who do not (Luthans et al. 2007). If you are a leader, you have no excuse not to use your team's strengths. They are the best resource you will ever have and they are being shamefully neglected. We should all be working strengths oriented.

More science? OK. Meta-studies are always great. The authors do the legwork for us by trawling through huge numbers of papers and collating their findings so that we do not have to. One of the largest such meta-analyses on strengths-based interventions that I am aware of was carried out by Asplund et al. (2016). It looked at 43 strengths studies conducted in 22 organizations across 45 countries. In total, 1.2 million individuals and 49,000 business units were compared. The results were mouthwatering. In companies and work organizations, where strengths-based interventions (e.g., strengths coaching, strengths training, etc.) had been implemented, improvement in almost all areas of the work experience was observed.

Those companies recorded up to 15 percent increases in employee engagement. Engaged employees, as we know, work better and are more productive (see Chapter 5) and that, in turn, leads to increased customer engagement (up to 6.9 percent). Companies which ran strengths-based programs reported a decrease in safety incidents of up to 59 percent. This statistic alone should be justification and motivation enough for business leaders to employ a strengths-oriented culture in their workplace but if it somehow does not excite them then the next two stats certainly will. Strengths-based companies are able to increase their sales from between 10.3 percent and 19.3 percent and increase their profits by up to 29.4 percent. Strengths orientation just works.

It makes people healthier, safer, better educated, and more satisfied in their job. It offers better career prospects, helps them be more productive, and brings in more cash. What is there not to love about strengths orientation?

Still not convinced? Need more proof? Another meta-study? OK. Here you go: Reilly (2014) cites a huge meta-analysis—this time of 339 research studies across 49 industries in 73 countries. In total, the studies included over 1.7 million people in over 80,000 departments and teams. The work (the ninth iteration of its kind) again found huge differences in multiple metrics between companies with large employee engagement and those struggling to engage their people. Absenteeism (41 percent down), staff turnover (59 percent down), safety incidents (70 percent down), quality defects (40 percent down) were all markedly reduced in companies with highly engaged employees, and productivity (17 percent), sales (20 percent), and profitability (21 percent) were all up. Strengths orientation just works.

I think that is enough about employee engagement for a while. Let us turn our attention to talent-oriented leadership and collaboration. A study from 2002 (Gallup) found that managers were 86 percent more likely of achieving project success if they adopted a strengths-based approach to their leadership. Moreover, Luthans et al. (2007) found that medium-sized companies may have the potential to increase their sales revenues by up to $12 million through strength-based leadership offered to their staff. Strengths orientation just works. Did I mention that already? What is more, an ever-growing body of evidence points to a direct link between employee well-being and performance (e.g., Zhu & Zhang 2014; Guest 2002). Strengths orientation just works. Compared with workers who do not get to actively engage with what they do best, people who have the opportunity to use their strengths at work are *six times* as likely to be motivated in their jobs and more than *three times* as likely to report having an excellent quality of life (Rath 2007).

Meanwhile, Cotton and Hart (2003) note the many organizational facets that can be negatively affected by poor employee well-being: increased number of compensation claims, decreased customer satisfaction, increased medical expenses, increased absenteeism due to sickness, and increased staff turnover. Furthermore, an overwhelming number of studies have shown a *direct* positive correlation between strengths use at work and higher performance (e.g. Dubreuil et al. 2014; Harzer & Ruch 2012, 2014; van Woerkom & Meyers 2015; van Wingerden & Van der Stoep 2018; van Woerkom & Maaike de Bruijn 2016). Indeed "there are several other large-scale meta-analyses consistently demonstrating the strong relationship between efficacy and the level of motivation and performance" (Luthans et al. 2007).

Studies show that people who know their strengths and can use them regularly are:

- happier, suffer less from depression, and have stronger mental health (Seligman et al. 2005);
- suffer less from the effects of stress (Wood et al. 2011);
- feel healthier, pursue a more healthy lifestyle and have more energy (Proyer et al. 2013);
- are more self-accepting and more self-confident (Govindji & Linley 2007);
- experience faster growth and development (Kirschbaum et al. 1982);
- are more proactive, creative, agile, and authentic at work (Dubreuil et al. 2014);

- find it easier to find meaning, pleasure and satisfaction at work (Harzer & Ruch, 2013); and
- are far more engaged at work (Crabb 2011).

I could go on all day, but I hope I have explained myself clearly. I trust you get the point. But do not take my word for it. Do some research of your own, if you are still skeptical. Over 500 studies have been conducted into the efficacy of strengths orientation.[2] Go to Google Scholar (or the academic search engine of your choice) and type in "strengths performance," "strengths-based leadership," "positive psychology at work," or some similar search term. You will be overloaded with study after study after study showing the efficacy of strengths-based collaboration and leadership in the workplace. Oh, and efficacy is just a cooler sounding word for "works." Strengths orientation is efficacious. Strengths orientation just works.

Whether it is simply waking up in the morning and deciding to put yourself in PFC and to employ a positive mindset or whether you actively identify with your talents and employ them in a strengths-oriented manner (more on that in the next chapters), the overwhelming evidence from the literature is that strengths orientation just ... well you get it.

---

[2]This is a nice starting point, if you are interested in reading more about strengths research: https://www.viacharacter.org/research/findings.

Your assumptions are your windows on the world. Scrub them off every once in a while, or the light won't come in.

Author, Isaac Asimov

CHAPTER 7

Assume a Virtue, If You Have It Not

Weakness Fixing—The Old, Conventional Assumptions

What will be essential, if you choose to adopt a strengths-based approach to your leadership and collaboration, is to switch your basic position from wherever it is now to a firm bee-glasses mindset of strengths orientation. The statistics and research findings are of little value if we are not prepared to make a genuine change in our lives. The problem here is that the phrase "mindset switch" is bandied around far too often these days, for my liking. People seem to think they need a mindset switch to lose a couple of pounds, change their Internet service provider, or buy a new pair of open shoes for the summer. Hogwash. Those aren't mindset switches, those are ideas; changes of habit, at best. A true mindset switch of the kind I am proposing here in this book can lead to paradigmatic transformation in both you and your results but it should not be taken lightly nor should you kid yourself of its ease. A change of mindset means questioning all your previous assumptions and stances on matters of human interaction and self-reflection and wiping the slate clean; prepared for a totally new paradigm. It means going back to how you have typically viewed and judged attitudes and being open to laying new pathways and to approaching challenges from a totally different cognitive starting point.

If I have whetted your appetite for true change, with the first chapters of this book, then stick around, you could be at the beginning of an exciting journey.

In the past, three conventional assumptions prevailed.

One: All Behaviors Can Be Learned

This beauty has been the basis of our education systems in the western world for hundreds of years. Our teachers, parents, or guardians told us that if we tried hard enough, we could do it. If we hit the books and burned the midnight oil, we could get any grade we wanted and achieve whatever we dreamt of. All we needed to do is want it—and we could get it. "If you dream it, you can achieve it," they promised. "You want to be an astronaut darling? No problem. Work hard and I'm sure you'll get there."

Baloney. Wanting something, no matter to what extent, will not get you there alone. Nor, sadly will mere hard graft. We have developed in such a way that some of us find it easier to learn certain things than others. If we could all learn everything … we would have done just that. If all behaviors could be learned, then there would be no excellence because we would all reach the same cognitive standard. I'm sorry to burst anyone's bubble here but we cannot learn anything we want. Some behaviors can be learned but many are impossible to learn. Even fewer are possible to master. We have been designed by the jaggedness principle to be significantly different from one another in order to solve humankind's multiple challenges. We are different for a reason and we learn (and can learn) differently for a reason. We learn differently so that we may develop into experts across multiple fields.

Two: The Best in a Role All Get There Exactly the Same Way

In the 1970s two of industry's greatest ever captains emerged. Both made tsunamic waves in the then burgeoning computer industry but both could not have been much more different from one another.

Bill Gates is a singularly focused and determined individual (Gilliard n.d.), who, as the head of Microsoft, worked long hours and expected the same dedication from his team (Rampton 2016). He believed in pursuing what you love and working in a field that stimulates you. He was a once-in-a-generation subject knowledge expert (software coding). He is shy and introverted, but polite and well mannered. He made decisions quickly, was autocratic and authoritarian, but encouraged his team to challenge the status quo with new ideas, although he often chastised them for what he deemed inaccurate assumptions or incorrect facts. He was not necessarily an ideas guy (for example, he bought the operating system BASIC, he did not actually design it), but his anticipation of trends was first rate. Since stepping back from direct control of Microsoft, he has set up the largest private foundation in the United States, the Bill and Melinda Gates Foundation, which aims to reduce poverty with multi-billion-dollar philanthropy.

At around the same time that Bill Gates was helping to build the computer software industry, a young college dropout was nudging his technologically more-gifted friend Steve Wozniak to develop the world's first attractive home computer in his parents' garage, so kick-starting the computer hardware industry. Steve Jobs became a fiery and fiercely ambitious leader, who surrounded himself with talent and pushed them to ever greater creative achievements (Isaacson 2012). This persuasive force that Jobs wielded was jokingly referred to as his "Reality Distortion Field after an episode of Star Trek in which aliens create a convincing alternative reality through sheer mental force" (Isaacson 2012). For example, he was once able to convince Steve Wozniak to design a game for Atari in four days, although Wozniak claimed he needed months. He has been described as "arrogant, dictatorial, and mean spirited" (Henson 2011), but was a genius with regard to design, did not care for customer or popular opinion "customers don't know what they want until we've shown them" (Isaacson 2012), and was an extroverted, salesman-supreme with the rare gift of the gab and unequaled persuasive, sales and pitching techniques (Isaacson 2011). In his private life, Gates was reclusive and stubborn. He estranged himself from family members for decades and lived in a sparsely decorated house, often sitting on the floor for lack of furniture.

Two men. Born around the same time. Growing up in the same period of history. Brought up in similar, American, middle-class backgrounds. Both entered the same infant (computer) industry, and both went on to become founding leaders of two of the most successful companies (by capital and market share) the world has ever seen. But, both worked and led in *very different ways*.

Jobs achieved greatness with silky communication skills and raw (but strengths-oriented) emotion, whereas Gates' drive, blinkered determination (he never let 21 years of legal challenges distract his work), and subject matter skills helped him lead his company to the top. Jobs' leadership gathered creative experts (he was never considered a computer expert himself) into his close circle of followers and drove them to excellence with ceaseless and seductive persuasion. Gates, on the other hand, founded his leadership philosophy on his own subject skills combined with tireless focus and attention to detail. He rarely included others in decision-making and micromanaged every aspect of business. However, his philanthropic nature was conspicuous in comparison to Jobs' troublesome private relationships. Two unforgettable leaders with two very distinct leadership styles.

The best in any role get there in very different ways.

Three: Weakness Fixing Leads to Success

We've already covered this old chestnut in Chapter 2. If you fix something—you still have the same something—it is just fixed. That is all that is different. To change anyone from something into something new, i.e. to promote development (toward success), you need to start with talent.

The Strengths-Oriented Assumptions

Out with the old and in with the new. The bee-glasses mindset requires a new set of assumptions. Make way for them. They are the foundation for everything else to come:

> Some behaviors can be learned but many are nearly impossible to learn. There is a difference between talent, skills, and knowledge (see Chapter 10).

> The best in a role deliver the same outcomes, but achieve success with different means.

> Fixing weaknesses prevents failure. Strengths building leads to excellence.

> Let us take a look at an organization that has adopted these strengths oriented assumptions.

Case Study—Sky

There are some companies which have, indeed already, embraced strengths orientation. A great example is Sky UK Ltd. Founded back in 1989 as satellite TV first came to the UK, Sky is newly owned by American telecommunications giant Comcast. Sky UK Ltd broadcast terrestrial satellite TV to around 12.5 million viewers through their set top boxes, offer on-demand services, and also provide high-speed Internet and a cell phone network. With a turnover of £13.585bn and pre-tax profits in 2018 of over £1bn, Sky UK Ltd is doing more than fine from the perspective of the money-makers and shareholders but it is the welfare of their staff which should interest you most. Sky as an employer goes above and beyond to make the working environment for its employers as welcoming as possible. Its aim is to make the working climate so efficacious that it attracts and, most importantly, holds onto the top talent (see Chapter 11 for more on these concepts). It does this with a collection of powerful yet mostly simple, positive-psychology ideas.

The headquarters of Sky UK Ltd is based in Osterley, just west of London. A huge, open campus connected by neat paths, perfectly kept lawns, trees, and activity areas. The usually casually dressed Sky staff (in total, there are around 30,000 globally) come and go as they like. They have access cards to open the gates and pay for snacks but there is no time clock. No one clocks in or out. Bosses don't ask where their subordinates are nor do they question what they are doing. Big Brother is not present. Let alone watching. "Everyone hot desks, and besides, we're all adults here. We all trust each other to figure it out," says Sky Marketing Manager, Caroline Clarke. "Hot desking" is the concept of choosing where, when, how, and with whom you work. There are no offices or set workstations in seven out of the eight buildings (only the broadcast crew work from set locations due to device login rights). The entire campus is a sprawl of sofas, beanbags, booths, tables of different heights, and ergonomic chairs. Everyone has a laptop and smart devices connected to the team collaboration tools and can dial-in from anywhere on-, or indeed off-, campus. Working from home (or the local café, or wherever) is fine, as long as the quality remains high.

It doesn't get loud and distracting because there are so many cozy corners and niches, that twos and threes can almost always find a spot to exchange. Conference rooms are only meant to be booked out if a group specifically needs access to a phone. Otherwise such ad hoc, hot desk meetings are actively encouraged, to drive collaboration.

> When someone with the expertise to help us with a particular issue is passing by, we simply grab them and pick their brains for a couple of minutes. On the flipside, having the meetings wherever we want them allows others to listen in and, if they feel they can add value, they do just that. They join in and contribute.

Clarke continues.

On the subject of collaboration, the snazzily named "Creative Solutions" department writes periodically to all staff, inviting them to open brainstorming sessions. At these meet-ups, staff can propose out-of-the box ideas, even if the client brief is not part of their day-to-day business.

New ideas are encouraged as they fuel creativity, give team members cross-field experience, and break up the potentially mundane day-to-day. The staff members at Sky are seen as contributors and talent, not as siloed workers. The company has even thought of a solution to those little, annoying tech problems: broken headphones, mouse, etc.: Staff simply go and help themselves to new kit from the IT tech vending machine which just charges back their department. But the employee-oriented philosophy doesn't stop there. The general welfare of the staff is so important to Sky that they offer a colorful catalogue of benefits (most for free, some for minimal, highly subsidized fees) to make the campus a workplace which people will want to come and work at, stay at and, once there, a place where they will be intrinsically motivated to deliver high performance.

There are four sit-down restaurants on-site. On the day of my interview, they were serving, among other things, 6 oz Rump steak, porcini sauce, watercress, scorched tomato and petit ratatouille for £3.87 (about 5 US Dollars). However, should the staff or visitors be hungry or thirsty for something else, there are seven or eight small cafés in addition to the various pop-up eateries scattered across the campus. Of course, there is something for all tastes: Halal, vegan, vegetarian, etc. and diners can reserve tables in comfort over their intranet. A top sushi chef pops in once per month to prepare fresh Japanese delicacies and there are regular cultural offerings at different times of the year, touting for example, Hindu food at Diwali.

An on-site hairdressers, a barbers, a nail salon, the largest gym of its kind in Europe and a spa mean that Sky team members can take the edge off and focus on themselves for an hour or two—and all of this can happen during work time. Staff simply get up and go, for example, to have their hair cut and return when they are finished. The overriding culture of trust ensures that no one asks or second guesses where anyone is. Table tennis tables, giant chess, free talks, network events, support groups (e.g., "Parents at Sky" or "Women at Sky"), etc. round off the huge palette of attractions available to staff and visitors.

But the organization has not only invested in cushions and dart boards to keep its people happy. Probably of even greater importance to the powers-at-be at Sky is the general well-being and professional and personal development of their people. A 6-monthly "People's Survey" inquires after staff mentality with concrete changes in process made, if the consensus desires. Answers to questions like "How are you being managed?" or "How do you feel at work?" allow staff to have a very real and active contribution to the (leadership) environment in which they work. The online magazine "Today at Sky" keeps all delegates up-to-speed on company internal matters as well as giving them a forum to make suggestions and propose ideas. But such open communication is not only possible online. Sky team members are encouraged to simply anecdotally approach and discuss their ideas with senior staff. There is no need for an "open-door policy." There are not even any doors.

On a more microlevel, each Sky staff member is invited to propose their own annual goals as part of their Personal Development Plan. These targets are set by the employee, not the employer, and are closely linked to one or more of the corporation's values:

Forward Looking and Restless
Customer Lead and Simplifying
Creative and Action-Oriented
Collaborative and Inclusive
Fair and Responsible.

In other words, employees decide which one of the values they would most like to focus on in the coming year and then set themselves personal development projects and make their year about that goal. The idea is pitched to the line manager who takes note and simply aligns with it. "It's your career. It's your development," says Caroline Clarke. Sky's transformational and progressive approach to leadership gives talent the space to try things and, more importantly, to grow. Sky employees, as a result, thrive from a reflective and reflexive mindset and an ownership of their development.

The cherry on the icing on the cake of strengths orientation at Sky UK Ltd is the cutely named "Sky Stars" program. This is not one of your classic performance-related pay (PRP) schemes whereby staff members get paid more if they sell X products or meet Y targets. "Sky Stars" is a promotion and acknowledgment of the excellence and humanity witnessed daily at Sky. Set up to supplement the classic, anecdotal, day-to-day: "Thank you, you did a great job" in the lift or at the coffee machine, Sky Stars is an online portal published for the whole workforce to see. Its use is super simple. If someone recognizes a good deed, a job well done, or that someone went "above and beyond," then they nominate the good turn and the best are celebrated on the intranet. That is it. No bonus. No extrinsic perk. No PRP. Just good old-fashioned (public) human respect. This simple but powerful tool helps garnish a culture of appreciation and, vitally, intrinsic motivation (see Chapter 8) that imperceptibly drives productivity. It costs nothing. There is no carrot and no stick—just co-workers wanting to get along and do right by one another.

The only downside to this incredible offer, quips Clarke, is "that people notice when you've had your hair dyed because you had a different color in the morning meeting!" Joking aside, the strengths-oriented and progressive culture at Sky just works. It attracts talent, keeps talent, gives people the space to stimulate creativity, and drives productivity and that productivity is mirrored in notable corporate fiscal success. What the leaders at Sky have realized is that such investment in staff and environment just pays off for both employee and employer.

The classic kickback I hear when I regale anyone who will listen to stories of strengths-based cultures such as Sky's is "Yeah. That's all well and good—but we are here to work, not play!" A young manager told me just recently for example that her first step upon becoming team leader was to take the mini table tennis table in a team member's office away because "it just isn't right to have fun at work!" She then went on to tell me about the disciplinary issues she is facing with that delegate. It seems he is unhappy at work and with her leadership and is going through various HR and workers' council channels to fight for the working environment he was happy with before her intervention. The whole debacle is draining both parties' time. Energy levels and focus have strayed far from the team or corporate goals.

My argument is not that table tennis tables will instantly bring your team's performance up, nor will sushi classes transform your staff, double-time, into highly motivated busy bees. A pool table might motivate one guy but distract the next. Some work better in the hubbub of open plan offices, while others prefer the peace and quiet of working from home. The chance to bounce in and out of meetings and subjects is not for everyone. I concede that. As Henry Ford once said: "You cannot please all the people, all of the time." But companies like Sky have realized that offering staff the chance to actually enjoy coming to work means that they do just that. They come to work and they work when they come.

There is a seismic shift happening right now in the hearts of some of our organizations.

The new workforce is looking for things like purpose, opportunities to develop, ongoing conversations, a coach rather than a boss, and a manager who leverages their strengths rather than obsessing over their weaknesses. They see work and life as interconnected (see chapter 11), and they want their job to be a part of their identity (Harter 2017).

This strengths-oriented purpose and work–life balance this new generation of talent so yearns for is attainable while also keeping the organization's (fiscal) goals alive.

If you are looking to flip the paradigm and move your workplace more toward a strengths-based climate, what steps should be taken? Harter (2017) suggests three ways to change organizational culture for the better toward a more strengths-oriented environment:

1. Audit

    Take a detailed, systematic look at your current performance management system. Dissect which parts of your system are working and which require attention. If fair (i.e., talent-driven) accountability and leadership coaching are already prevalent, then keep that ball rolling and support its further development. By the same token, if elements of your operations work against productive conversations, intrinsic motivation, and mutual respect, then work needs to be done in those areas.

2. Train

    Ideally the whole organization would be introduced to the strengths approach but, at the very least, junior managers need to benefit from effective performance development interventions. Building a mindset from the foundations up is the only way to ensure its long-term, genuine survival. Managers need to be schooled in transformational conversations and coached on recognizing and rewarding talent. They need to become experts on creating an environment whose sole purpose is to get people into Prefrontal Cortex (PFC).

3. Build

    Construct a scientific system to ensure that the right people become a manager. You want leaders who can naturally deal with the idiosyncrasies of delegating and transformationally communicating with people. Some individuals are more naturally gifted at developing people toward high performance than others. You need leaders who believe in and live the strengths-oriented mindset.

Motivation is a fire from within. If someone else tries to light that fire under you, chances are it will burn very briefly.

Bestselling author, Stephen Covey

CHAPTER 8

Intrinsic Motivation

Does the basketball player, who gets paid US$100,000 per week, score twice as many points as his teammate whose agent only negotiated their player a $50,000 contract? Does the fat-cat CEO who sets herself up with a US$6 million annual salary plus bonus (paid out irrespective of whether or not targets are met) generate US$5 million more than a CEO paid US$1 million? (Ariely 2008). Do graphic designers create more innovative conceptions if they are threatened with redundancy if the next design is not groundbreaking?

Think of a task that you do not enjoy doing. When you do this particular task, do you often watch the clock, counting the seconds until it is finished? It brings you no joy, and you do not consider that you are very good at it. Indeed, others (including your superior) have given you the feedback that you are not good at it. They watch over you closely to see whether or how badly you complete the task. Would you perform this task better (i.e., deliver souped-up performance, resulting in improved overall quality), if I offered to pay you more than you usually get paid for it or threatened to fire you if you do not perform? Many scientific teams over the years have looked at just these questions: Does more money motivate us to be more productive? Does fear of punishment drive us to better performance? In other words, does the proverbial carrot dangled in front of the donkey or the threat of the stick smacking down on its backside motivate the animal to deliver eminence?

The business world has predominantly worked on the premise of the carrot and stick since ... well since forever. Many companies expect top performance, staff retention, and loyalty from their staff, but motivate solely extrinsically (Luthans 2011). Organizations sometimes offer only short-term contracts, fleeting periods of notice, or prolonged probation periods designed to drive hard work for fear of redundancy. Some offer benefits (for example, dental care) only after certain milestones have been achieved or after X years of service or set future pay-rises only when recorded achievements have been triggered. The fear of redundancy is very real for millions of employees (irrespective of whether this is voiced directly or implied more subtly), and huge numbers of people working today have success-related pay schemes built into their remuneration packages, whereby they have the potential to be paid more as long as they, their team, or the corporation achieves certain targets. Classic examples would be a salesperson, who, for every 1,000 gizmos he or she sells, earns €5,000 more for the team, which, at the end of the fiscal year, upon reaching its targets of units sold, splits a (taxable) bonus pot. This form of extrinsic motivation (i.e., motivation by tangible, outside factors) has created a high-pressure scenario in which we have been led to believe that, if we work harder, we will be paid more or at least not get fired. In many cases, such motivation does lead staff to toil and graft more, but evidence suggests that it does not bolster distinction.

A paradigm exists where staff overexert themselves to achieve externally set goals in pursuance of their bonus payout. Meanwhile, many others work long hours to impress management, often clocking-up large accounts of (sometimes unpaid) overtime to avoid the dreaded sack and resulting unemployment. For generations, an assumed staple of professional motivation—the carrot and the stick—does not actually work. Extrinsic motivation does sometimes make people work more but it does *not* make them work better.

Despite overwhelming evidence to the contrary, generations of leaders, one after the other, have continued to tread the same path, and largely with the same unsatisfactory results. Many people, when a strategy fails at the first attempt, employ exactly the same game plan again and again. It is time to break the mold, listen to what science is telling us about motivation, and rouse a culture of intrinsic motivation that spawns passionate high performance.

The Truth about Intrinsic Motivation

The science world has shown in copious studies that it disagrees with the business world's view that an offer of the carrot or threat of the stick expedites excellence. Extrinsic motivation does not lead to higher performance. It may, in some cases, lead to longer working hours and burnout (Lemyre et al. 2006; ten Brummelhuis et al. 2011; Bakker & Costa 2014), but it does not lead to better performance. And, at the end of the day, what is our goal as leaders if not to strive to develop our team and to aid them in getting the best out of themselves? In this section of the chapter, I will share with you the findings from a number of seminal studies, which vociferously suggest that leaders should be motivating in an entirely different way.

Glucksberg, with two experiments (1962 and 1964), was one of the first in the modern era to investigate the correlation between extrinsic (in this case, financial) rewards and the quality and speed of completing conceptual, cognitive tasks. In other words, if I pay someone for it, then will they complete a task better than a person who has not been paid? Such positions are known as if-then frameworks (Winne & Hadwin 2008). In the study, Glucksberg asked two groups of participants to solve the cognitive performance test first designed by Karl Duncker in the 1930s. It is known as Duncker's candle problem (Duncker & Lee 1945).

Dunker's candle problem goes like this: You observe some items on a table (Figure 8.1), near a wooden wall. Some tacks, a candle, and a set of matches. Your task is to firmly attach the candle to the wall, making sure the wax does not drip onto the table, using only the objects in front of

Figure 8.1 The candle experiment

you. How might you solve this puzzle? You cannot pin the candle to the wall with the tacks; the tacks are too short; the candle is too thick. What is more, the candle wax breaks off when you stick a pin in it. So that is a no go. You can heat the candle with a match until it drips and then use the melted wax as adhesive to stick the candle to the wall, but you will find that the candle is too heavy for the wax to hold it.

There is only one way to solve the conundrum, and most people stumble across it after a few minutes of consideration. Take the tacks out of the box, pin the box to the wall with the tacks, stand the candle in the box, and light it with a match. It seems so easy once you know the solution, right? But many of us do not quickly recognize the box as contributing. We appreciate the box only as a holder for the tacks, seldom as a distinct tool in itself. Or, indeed, some of us do not notice the box at all. This is called functional fixedness (Glucksberg & Weisberg 1966). That is, only seeing something in one state and not appreciating its potential other uses. Duncker's candle problem was repeated by other scientists and with much larger sample groups, always with the same results (Adamson 1952).

Interestingly, if subjects are shown the tacks lying on the table outside of the now empty box, then the candle problem can be solved much more quickly. People almost immediately recognize the box as being helpful in the task and a potential holder for the candle, and there is little or no functional fixedness, so the task is easy. More on this later. What Glucksberg found was that, if he incentivized people to solve the initial candle problem faster by pledging to pay the fastest 20 percent of people US$5 and the fastest of all US$20 (adjusted for inflation that's about around US$40 and US$160, respectively, today, not bad for a few minutes thought), then they, in fact, were *slower* than people who had not been paid to decipher the same challenge. On average, it took the group that was offered an extrinsic reward 3.5 minutes longer than those who were offered nothing. Glucksberg then restaged the experiment with one significant difference. This time he set the tacks up outside of the box and left the empty box in view on the table. This time around the incentivized group was faster than the other group.

So what does this all mean? It shows us that reward-based if-then signatures apply with straightforward tasks, but when assignments require more advanced cognitive processing, then promise of extrinsic reward can actually be counterproductive and produce worse performance. This seems to go against all we think we know about motivation. It seems to make little common sense, and yet, it is accurate. Dan Pink explains it best: "Rewards, by their very nature, narrow our focus. That's helpful when there's a clear path to a solution. They help us stare ahead and race faster. But 'if-then' motivators are terrible for [cognitive processing] challenges like the candle problem" (Pink 2011). In fact Pink later goes further by adding that "'if-then' motivators that are the staple of most businesses often stifle, rather than stir, creative thinking" (Pink 2011). As this experiment shows, the rewards narrowed people's focus and blinkered them from the big picture. It goes against decades of assumed logic, but extrinsic motivation does not improve high-level cognitive performance (i.e., exactly what we expect from our teams every day). But, one swallow does not make a summer. The above constitutes just the result from one guy's experiments. What do other scholars have to say about motivation?

One could argue that the reward amounts in Glucksberg's study were too small to strongly affect subjects' motivations or levels of effort. In the United States, US$5 is a small amount of money, but in some countries, it carries far greater value due to different economies and buying power. So what might happen, if we dangle larger carrots?

A group of U.S.-based academics led by Professor Dan Ariely (2009) investigated the effect of extrinsic motivation, in a similar study to Glucksberg, but took their study instead to Madurai, India. With the price of living and earnings-to-value ratio markedly different in India, significant rewards could be offered without blowing the academics' budget. They got a group of participants to complete a series of tasks that tested their motor skills, concentration levels, and creativity. The subjects were split into three groups, and all were set certain targets in each of the exercises. About 33 percent of the group was told that they would be remunerated with a small monetary reward (4 rupees: around 50¢ or equivalent to about one day's pay) if they reached their performance targets. Another third would receive a medium-sized reward (around US$5, equivalent to about 2 weeks' pay) and the last group was promised a very large reward (about US$50: around 5 months' pay) if they met their targets. The results, again, contradicted popular wisdom on motivation. The group paid the largest extrinsic rewards fared the worst in eight out of the nine exercises. And remember, 50 bucks would not feel like 50 bucks to the rural Indians in this experiment. Think of what you earn in 5 months, i.e., nearly half your yearly salary. Now ask yourself how that amount would weigh on your mind if you were offered it for solving just a couple of silly classroom games. Extrinsic rewards distract—they don't motivate.

In another study, Bernd Irlenbusch at the London School of Economics (2009) looked at over 50 financially incentivized payment schemes and found that, rather than motivate positive behavior, pay-for-performance plans actually stymie effectiveness. "We find that financial incentives may indeed reduce intrinsic motivation and diminish ethical or other reasons for complying with workplace social norms such as fairness. As a consequence, the provision of incentives can result in a negative impact on overall performance" (Irlenbusch cited in Morningstar 2012). Leaders commonly reward key performance indicator (KPI)-derived and measurable performance, and not creativity. Consequently, employees often offer up this type of more-of-the-same performance rather than creative thinking (Eisenhower & Shanock 2003).

As we have seen, motivation narrows focus, and this narrowing—often caused by blinkered attempts to achieve goals—also stunts creativity and excellence. That in turn can precipitate unethical, untrustworthy behavior, risk-taking, and decreased cooperation. The staff sees only the goal and may employ any means to justify the end. Imagine your corporation announces that the salesperson with the best stats at the end of the year will be given a huge bonus. One night, shortly before the year's end, one of the team finds themself alone in the office. They have access to the main computer and only have to change a three to a four on the sales charts to put themselves in pole position to win that bonus. Might they be motivated to do such an unethical act? Might the carrot intended to inspire excellence, actually inspire deception?

Extrinsic motivation has similarly negative effects on creativity. Harvard academic Professor Theresa Amabile (1996) set up a clever study where she had 23 artists present 20 paintings each to a panel of art experts. Half were commissioned and half noncommissioned. The panel judged the commissioned paintings (i.e., those that were ordered for payment) as "significantly less creative" (Amabile, cited in Pink 2011) than the ones that were simply created for the artist's own pleasure. What is more, the artists noted their lack of joy and the creative restraint that they felt when producing work on demand.

This is known as the Sawyer effect (Ariely et al. 2006): Mark Twain's famous hero Tom Sawyer, once lumbered with the chore of whitewashing a huge fence in the midday sun had the brainwave of persuading his friends to take over his work by convincing them that it was a rare opportunity to be able to do such a task, and that many had previously wanted to. As he sat on a nearby tree stump watching his peers gladly complete the task, which he had only minutes before hated, he mused that "Work consists of whatever a body is obliged to do," and that "Play consists of whatever a body is not obliged to do." If we present something as work by offering a reward, then people we are trying to motivate instinctively recognize it as undesirable. The potential issue here for leaders is that we also set a precedent. If I ask you to complete a task that you do not want to do and you say no, maybe I could offer to reward you for it. The thing is I will now have to reward you every time in the future, to the same level, to bag your compliance.

We have looked at the carrot, but what about the stick? Surely the threat of punishment compels people to follow rules. Doesn't it? Gneezy and Rustichini (2000) observed a daycare facility post a sign to warn delinquent parents that if they turned up late to pick up their child they would in future be faced with a fine. After the notice was posted, twice as many parents on average as before arrived late to collect their sons and daughters. The threat of the fine, hoping to hone parents' feeling of responsibility, and prime their behavior, served as the opposite and encouraged unpunctuality. The fine, instead of motivating good attitude, had turned a human relationship between the parents and teachers into a transaction. Now, the parents could simply *buy* extra time, if they needed it (Suvorov 2003).

The carrot and the stick do not work. To stimulate cognition, creativity, and desire, people require intrinsic motivation. Dan Pink cutely sums up the dangerous side effects of extrinsic motivation in his seven deadly carrot and stick flaws:

1. They can extinguish intrinsic motivation.
2. They can diminish performance.
3. They can crush creativity.
4. They can crowd out good behavior.

5. They can encourage cheating, shortcuts, and unethical behavior.
6. They can become addictive.
7. They can foster short-term thinking.

Now, I would like to make something clear at this point. I am not saying money is not nice. It helps us fund our lives and keep our families safe and warm, and that is doubtless a good thing. I am not saying we should stop remunerating our staff. I am not saying people do not work for money and enjoy earning, having, and spending money. What I am saying is that, after a certain geo-socially acceptable level of remuneration that is comparable in that industry, people are content in their roles. To encourage best-in-class performance, out-of-the-box thinking, and state-of the-art creativity on top, leaders need to plug in intrinsic motivation for their teams.

High-Performance Motivation

If we cannot coerce preeminence out of our teams with the proverbial carrot dangle or with the intimidation of the stick slap, how can we get our guys to perform? Luckily, many experts have looked at the subject of intrinsic motivation, and some have proposed starting blocks to help employees discover their own intrinsic drivers. At the first reflective stage, intrinsic motivators can be divided into 12 categories (see the following table). This list of drivers should by no means be construed as conclusive, but as a helpful suggestion of the types of areas one should look at to glean intrinsic motivation. This list has been compiled from eight models on human needs and desires (Table 8.1).

I make that 48 drivers that scientists suggest may intrinsically motivate people to work better. The problem with this list, as I see it, is twofold:

1. Most of your team, when shown this list, will probably highlight different selections from the table as their own personal drivers. Helping each member of your group identify their own motivators may prove fiddly.
2. Your leadership would have to be so situational as to be microscopic in order to constantly seek to motivate all at their own, individual level.

Table 8.1 Common intrinsic and extrinsic motivators

Responsibility Loyalty, integrity, principles, values	Autonomy Freedom, independence	Curiosity Learning something new, collecting experience, wanting to understand, thirst for knowledge	Social Recognition Social acceptance, affiliation, recognition in social networks
Well-being Relaxation, emotional security, without stress and fear, inner peace, calmness	Ownership and Wealth Accumulation of material goods, property, assets, wealth	Performance and Competence Leadership, influence, ambition, success, effectiveness of one's own actions	Fairness Social justice, social involvement, compassion
Collegiality and Care Friendship, meeting, social contacts, proximity, helping	Status Social standing, title, privileges, exclusiveness, prestige	Challenge Competition, rivalry	Structure and Security Stability, clarity, good organization, structure, detail

Thankfully, Pink (2010) has provided us with a much simpler, concise model of intrinsic motivation that is both easy to recognize for the employee and manageable for a leader. According to Pink, we, as leaders, have a responsibility to create an environment where our subordinates, with our support, can blossom in a climate of trust and be purely and intrinsically motivated by giving them just three motivational foci: autonomy, mastery, and purpose.

Autonomy

Let your people work when and how they want to. When leading your team, instill the why in them, but leave the how up to them. Entrepreneur and multiple company CEO Jeff Gunther calls this ROWE: results-only work environment. In ROWEs, it is irrelevant when people show up for work, where they work, and with whom they collaborate. It is only important that they deliver results. Give talented people the tools they need, but also, critically, the space they crave to work autonomously, and they will be driven to achieve for achievements sake. No carrot in

---

[1]3 Hierarchy of Needs: Maslow (1971); ERG Theory: Alderfer (1969); System of Needs: Murray (1938); Life Motives: Reiss (2004); Theory of Motivation (Kasser & Ryan 1993), Self-Determination Theory: Ryan and Deci (2000); Needs Theory: McClelland (1951).

sight. Teleworking, flexitime, and spatial decentralization have all been shown to positively affect industrial performance (Martínez Sánchez et al. 2007). If your company regulations allow, then let your team off the leash, transactionally set goals together with them, and let them work as autonomously as possible.

Mastery

In short, people achieve best when they are doing what they love. When we work autonomously, we are engaged and driven to want to improve. Sadly, this engagement is lacking in so many modern offices and workplaces. According to a McKinsey study, in some countries, no more than a few percent of the workforce claims to be engaged in their work all the time (Kirkland 2009). But, outside of the workplace, it proliferates. Mastering a challenging skill, be it painting that landscape, climbing that rock face, or building that tree house—we would all do any of these and more stimulating, fascinating, challenging tasks for no money, just for the thrill of being able to say afterward: "I did that." Millions of us take dance classes or learn musical instruments or uncover the artistry behind creative writing or sculpture, or whatever. We do all these things for free. Amateur musicians spend hours practicing their scales because it makes them better, and that development of mastery puts them in reward mode and is powerfully addictive. In such pursuits, the activity is reward in itself. Motivation and happiness guru Csikszentmihalyi called these autotelic experiences (from the Greek for self [auto] and the Greek for goal [telos]). He later shortened the word to the far pithier: flow. One simple question: why don't your people deserve as much autotelic experience at work as they have in their private lives? Just think what they might achieve if they were in flow every day.

Purpose

If you were to draw a graph with time (let us say the last 100 years) on the x-axis and numbers of engaged workers and numbers of people volunteering for good causes on the y-axis, you would see the engagement line steadily heading down, but being intersected by the volunteerism line rising exponentially. In the last couple of generations, the numbers of people searching for a purpose in charities, clubs, schools, political parties, good causes, social or environmental groups, and so on has continued to rise, while worker engagement falls year on year. This suggests that people are searching for something in their voluntary contributions that they are simply not finding at work. What can we learn from this social activity?

A survey commissioned in the United Kingdom in 2015 found that 58 percent of full-time staff (and 70 percent of part-time staff) feel that they have little or no influence at work, and 59 percent think they have no control over big business (UK.coop 2015). Many seem disillusioned with the business world they work in and feel their contribution changes little. Many recognize little purpose in their work. Such industrial disenchantment is one of the main reasons why we have seen such a dramatic rise in cooperative-styled start-ups in recent years (uk.coop). A cooperative (coop) can take many forms, but recently, we have seen numerous not-for-profit or profit-sharing organizations, that is worker cooperatives managed or owned by the staff, and consumer cooperatives that are managed by their customers, popping up. What is most intriguing is not so much that many seem drawn to businesses operating under a cooperative framework (as employees and as customers), but that such organizations are so successful. A 2007 study found that 90 percent of the coops were still operating after 5 years, compared with 3 to 5 percent of traditional corporations. The 30,000 cooperative companies in the United States in 2009 helped create over two million jobs and contributed over US$150 million to the U.S. economy. People seem to want coops to work. Coop members share a vision that drives them to not let them fail.

Now, I am not proposing you all quit your jobs and go set up coops tomorrow. That is not the message here. The coop, like any other company form, has its pros and cons. Of interest here is the drive, connection, and motivation that is often shown by coop members. They identify a purpose in their work; they recognize direction; and they are prepared to invest significant time and energy (irrespective of material gains) to contribute to that shared success. We can certainly learn something for our capitalist companies about the power of purpose as a motivator from such constructs.

A leader needs to know his strengths as a carpenter knows his tools, or as a physician knows the instruments at her disposal.

The founder of the Strengths Movement, Don Clifton

CHAPTER 9

Identifying Strengths

Gallup CliftonStrengths™

As briefly mentioned in Chapter 1, one of the best known and probably the most used strengths identification assessments is the Gallup Strengths Finder, also called the Clifton Strengths Finder (CSF) or CliftonStrengths™ (Harms 2017).[1] It was developed by the American research organization Gallup, who are probably more famous for their polls (Freeburg 2014) but in the 1990s, under the leadership of educational psychologist Donald Clifton, the CSF was born out of over 2 million interviews conducted to identify talented staff (Schreiner 2006). The tool itself was first introduced as an addendum to the 2001 book Now Discover Your Strengths and is now included in the updated version of the book StrengthsFinder 2.0, which was first published in 2007, and is routinely one of the best-selling business books (Freeburg 2014). The CSF can also be accessed using a code directly on the Gallup website.

As of June 2020, over 23 million people have taken the test worldwide. It is an online self-assessment designed to assess "fixed universal personal-character attributes" (Wikipedia) and to help the taker to identify 34 "signature themes" (Lopez et al. 2005), where they instinctively have the greatest potential to develop their naturally "recurring patterns of thought, feeling, and behavior" (Freeburg 2014) into strengths (see Chapter 10).

It does this by inviting the taker to choose one option each from 177 ipsative paired questions. When you input the code found at the back of

---

[1] I'd like to make very clear that I have absolutely no agreements (financial or otherwise) with any of the assessments mentioned in this book. I purchased the full version of all of them as part of the research for this book.

the book into the online tool, it shows you pairs of optional potential self-descriptors, one after the other, that appear to represent two poles on a continuum. You have 20 seconds on each page to decide which descriptor to pick. You are instructed to choose the one that you deem most accurate in describing your instinctive way of acting or thinking. An ipsative pair might look something like:

> I like to learn from actions in the past—vs.—I often think about what the future will look like

If you cannot decide between the two, then you also have the option to click in the middle, so telling the system, that you have chosen neither.

The idea is that the limited time available for each question nudges you toward making an instinctive, gut decision and prevents you from reflecting on what you might consider the socially best-accepted response. "Which option would Gandhi or Mother Theresa choose?" is a question that you should not be asking yourself, when taking the test. It should be your spontaneous, core response. Hence the time pressure.

Upon completion of all the question pairs, the system calculates your responses and spits out your 34 talent themes (compiled in four categories) in order of their prevalence or weighting. In other words, the talent theme listed as number 1 for you will be the one that the system deems the most prevailing one; i.e., the one that you identify with as being a very common way of acting. When you look at your 34th theme you will probably say: "yeah, that's not how I act at all!"

An immediate advantage of the test is as a view into how different we all are. When you take the assessment, you can elect to receive either only a presentation of your top five talent themes or, for a few dollars more, a rundown of all 34. The chances of a respondent having their 34 themes in the same order as someone else are 33 million to one and the chances of sharing the same top five are 278,256 to one (McCarville 2020). Due to their individual nature, the results illustrate an excellent starting point for self-reflection as they display the powerful cognitive diversity in us all.

But the virtues of the CSF don't end there. In addition to the list of talent themes, the tool also provides the testee with individualized report texts, constructed using an algorithm based on the exact responses to the 177 questions. To reflect on their own talents and to begin the journey of appreciating how better understanding their talents could help them to be more productive and work more positively, respondents can then read these texts and compare their suggestions to their own self-assessment of how they do things.

Although an enormous amount of studies has been conducted on the methodology, on the results, and on the validity of the test, a large proportion of the research is proprietary to Gallup and so not available for citation. What is more, Gallup have trademark and copyrighted all of their work, so it is not even possible for me to describe to you what your report will look like after you have taken the test—i.e., which talent themes you have.[2] I find that a pity, because I would simply love to have been able to share with you the genius of the assessment and its stunning validity.[3]

Personally, my experience of the test has been singularly positive. It genuinely changed my approach to life and work, after I took it myself and I have spoken with literally thousands who have been similarly moved and inspired.

I can only remember one delegate ever who, after a couple of sessions of reflection, still felt that what the test had proposed to him did not represent the talents he identified with. Axel from Sweden was apoplectic to find the talent for looking into the future in his top 5 (Gallup call this futuristic). He rarely planned for or cared about the future, he argued. What was more he certainly wasn't a time traveler or space man or any other such nonsense. I understood his woes and suggested that he spend the remaining time in the workshop reflecting on and discussing his other four talents in his top five and that he park the reflection on futuristic for a few days. We returned several weeks later, in module 2 of the leadership program he was a participant on, and I asked him how he now stood on his alleged talent futuristic. Still the same he retorted. No change. He still didn't identify as a futuristic person. Ripple dissolve and I get a message 6 months later over social media from Axel. After months

---

[2] I submitted requests to Gallups to be allowed to share its brilliant assessment with you here in more detail, but my application, sadly, was denied.

[3] I strongly recommend that you check out the publications for yourself on the CSF and on its statistical validity in particular. A simple search on scholar search engines for "strengths finder" should suffice.

of soul-searching, coaching, and repeated requests from him for feedback from his peers, he had an epiphany, that he did indeed have a strong pro-clivity for futurism. His focus is almost always on the deadline, he wrote. He is a sucker for dates and achieving goals and this fixation on due dates drove much of how he approached his work. That was how his talent for futurism materialized itself. Something, maybe the science fiction sound to the word, had misled him. He now identifies wholeheartedly with his futuristic talent. In my experience, not only Axel can benefit from the CliftonStrengths™ as a very powerful tool for fueling self-reflection.

Other Strength Assessment Tools

If you get the opportunity, I can only recommend that you take a strengths test. It can be a life-changing experience for many and it only costs, at the most, a few bucks. But CliftonStrengths™ is not your only option.

The HIGH5 Test

Over 1 million people have taken the HIGH5 test. Its founders want to allow people to learn about their top strengths without having to pay for them. Access to their technical reports is also freely available and citable. The free version allows you to see your top five strengths but to access your full report you will need to pay $29.99. Its reputation appears to be growing, in particular in business, where 90 percent of the Fortune 500 companies have already used it to discover their people's strengths. HIGH5 grew out of the research from self-proclaimed *Chief Happiness Officer* Dmitry Golubnichy. His work looked at the happiness of over 8 million people in over 160 countries. Golubnichy's 2017 book invites its readers to try a whacky or fun "happiness inducing suggestion" every day for 100 days and then rate their happiness every 25 days of the chal-lenge. According to Golubnichy, people report being 19 percent happier at the end of the challenge.

The mechanics of the test differ in a few ways from the CSF. Its tak-ers get to choose how they feel about two statements anywhere on a scale denoting the spectrum of emotions from "strongly disagree" to "strongly agree" as opposed to the three selection options in the CliftonStrengths™

assessment. The test is also slightly shorter—it only takes around 20 minutes to complete and if you decide to change your mind, you can click back and adjust your response whereas with the CliftonStrengths™, once you've clicked your response to a question, it is locked in. There is no going back. Another difference is that HIGH5 takers are not pressured to respond with a time limit. They can take as much time as they like to consider each question. A clever feature unique to the HIGH5 test is the ability to invite your peers to anonymously give you feedback on their perception of your strengths and to compare your strengths against those of, say, your teammates.

HIGH5's understanding of strengths is similar to Gallup's, although they don't appear to differentiate between talent and strength:

HIGH5 strengths are recurring patterns of thoughts, decisions, actions, and feelings that satisfy 5 major criteria:

1. You feel natural at using and developing your ability;

2. You get positive energy when using your strengths;

3. Others also perceive it as your strength;

4. It goes along with your values and understanding of a strength;

5. It satisfies your inner needs.

The questions reflect those criteria. By way of an example, here are some real questions from the test:

I find it hard to accept someone's wishful thinking instead of proven and grounded facts.

Others describe me as a spontaneous and easily adaptable person.

It's natural for me to find the positive in every situation.

Upon finishing the test (and paying to peek behind the paywall), HIGH5 presents you with your 20 talents ranked into four groups of five each: The five strengths upon which you should focus, five that you should leverage, five that require navigation, and the last five which HIGH5 suggests delegating away.

VIA-IS

Values in Action Inventory of Strengths (VIA-IS) is maybe the least imaginatively named of our strengths evaluations but it is the one with the most readily available supporting academic research. The survey is provided by the Ohio-based nonprofit organization the VIA Institute on Character whose mission it is to "help people change their lives by tapping into the power of their own greatest strengths… to advance both the science and practice of character, and empower those on their strengths-building journey" (viacharacter.org). To this end, they provide both the assessment, simple reports on the results and access to relevant strengths research for free. The VIA also conducts a large amount of strengths research themselves and, unlike other strengths test providers, all of their findings can be cited and reproduced.

Over 7.5 million people have so far taken the VIA-IS test which, like the HIGH5 test, is free. Unlike HIGH5, the VIA-IS even allows you to see all (in this case 24) of your strengths in order, for no fee, but to receive more detailed explanations of your strengths together with tips and tricks to leverage them, a payment of $20[4] is required. Answering the one hundred questions only takes about 10 minutes, which makes it the speediest out there. Interesting for you with time-keeping talents out there? You could take more time if you wanted to, as you are given no deadline per question and you can choose to express your responses in one of the following five ways: "Very Much Like Me, Like Me, Neutral, Unlike Me, Very Much Unlike Me." The questions have a similar feel to those in the other two tests already discussed. Here are a couple of actual questions used in the assessment:

I always keep my promises.

I always speak up in protest when I hear someone say mean things.

I try to add some humor to whatever I do.

---

[4]For a small extra payment, the VIA will also put together a tailor-made pack of relevant research for you.

StrengthsProfile.com

StrengthsProfile (formerly known as Realise2) rounds off our mini-presentation of the online strengths tests available today. It was designed by a leading expert in the field of positive psychology Alex Linley who together with his founding team proudly claim 100 combined years of experience in strengths research.

Their website and tool is, in my opinion, the slickest of the lot. It is provided by the organization Capp and has been available since 2005. StrengthsProfile identifies 60 signature strengths, making it by far the largest span of distinct signature themes. You can see your top seven of those (and a couple of other goodies, see below) for $14 or download a detailed report for $60. To get your profile, you have to answer 180 questions. That makes it the longest of the tests. It took me about 45 minutes to complete. You can go back and see or even change your responses at any time, which is a helpful feature if you think you might have mis-clicked and there is also no time pressure. The test is divided into three parts: The first 60 questions ask you to self-assess how successful you are at certain tasks. Linley calls this "Performance" and typical questions look like this:

How successful are you at...

...Making sure that you never waste time?

...Building rapport with people quickly and easily?

You can choose from one of seven responses to each of these first 60 questions: "Very unsuccessful, Unsuccessful, Slightly unsuccessful, Neither successful nor unsuccessful, Slightly successful, Successful, or Very successful." The next 60 questions investigate your emotions (StrengthsProfile call this "energy") when using your strengths and each begins with "How do you feel when…." At this stage in the test, your choices change to: "Very drained, Drained, Slightly drained, Neither energized nor drained, Slightly energized, Energized, Very energized." This approach to varying the design of the questions and the possible responses resonated well with me personally, as I felt like I had a greater understanding of the questions' intentions, compared against the other three tests. A couple of energy questions look like this:

How do you feel when you…

…Remain balanced and self-assured in difficult situations?

…Bring a structure and order to things by organizing them?

The third and final chunk of the test (again 60 questions) probes your use of your strengths. You are asked: e.g.

How often do you find yourself noticing or remembering the small differences between people that make them who they are?

How often do you find yourself keeping going until you succeed when faced with problems or difficulties?

Your options are: "Extremely rarely, Rarely, Infrequently, Neither frequently nor infrequently, Frequently Often, or Extremely often."

After the somewhat exhausting process, the system spits out your top seven "Realized strengths," as well as four of your "unrealized strengths," four themes which StrengthsProfile describes as "learned behaviors," and even three of your "weaknesses." This makes it the only strengths procedure that I know of that even ever uses the word "weakness," let alone highlights yours. Why you only see some of your 60 strengths in each category is also unclear. The report pages and sundry resources on the site seem snazzy and comprehensive enough, though.

I have completed all four of the surveys mentioned above and my personal experience of them was similar. The workings differ slightly from test to test but the principle is the same: Answer some questions honestly about how you experience your attitude to life and work and you will be presented with a list of signature strengths individual to you. Each organization uses its own vocabulary—compare from across the HIGH5, Strengths Profile, and VIA-IS:

- "action," "zest," and "catalyst"
- "fairness," "equality," and "peacekeeper" or
- "curiosity," "love of learning," and "philomath"

but the principle is the same: I can use the identified signature themes to begin a journey of self-reflection, transparently and systematically. Taking a strengths survey is an experience that I can only recommend, if nothing else, as it forces you to stop for a moment and think about yourself for a few minutes (Yes, you are allowed!). Take one or some of the tests. Take them all, for all I care. But if and when you do, let me know about your feelings about their results? Drop me a line.[5] I'd love to hear from you about your strengths test experiences.

Self-Assessment/Getting Feedback

If you don't currently have access to a test code, then that does not exclude you from reflecting on your strengths. If I asked you the following questions, which would you answer with yes?

- Do you make to-do lists?
- Do you make to-do lists for private events and tasks, at the weekend?
- Do you have to tidy your home, before you can relax?
- Are you sometimes accused of being too nice?
- Are you sometimes accused of not being nice enough?
- Do you organize your clothes or books according to color?
- Do you doodle, when you are on the phone?
- Do you prefer to listen to music when you revise, learn, or read? Or do you prefer silence?
- Do you sometimes repeatedly press the button to "remind" the lift that you would like to go?

If 100 people are currently reading this book, then I reckon that we would have 100 different sets of responses. Our cognitive difference has already been discussed in Chapter 4 but I further posit that most of us *know* what we are good at (at least regarding some of our talents) already, without the need for an online test. We know how we like things. We know how we approach challenges and tasks. We know whether we feel

---

[5]matt@mattbeadle.com, https://www.linkedin.com/in/mattbeadle/

comfortable or uncomfortable in certain social or communication settings. We can all remember newly learned skills coming easily to us and we have all been in flow at least some time in our lives.

I will go into this phenomenon more in Chapter 10 but, for now, remember that a good old-fashioned chunk of self-reflection can go a long way to a strengths-oriented mindset. Next time you get the chance, grab yourself a piece of paper and something to write with and jot down:

- things you find easy,
- things you enjoy doing,
- ways that you instinctively tend to address problems,
- occasions when time seemed to fly by as you enjoyed your work.

Most of those instances were almost certainly related to your talents in some way. Use any language you like. Call your strength stamina, determinedness, never-say-die-style, focus. Heck, you can even call it Steve, if you want. But take a moment to identify your talents. Something tells me that you might not think about how great at some things you are often enough. Most of us do not usually sit around patting ourselves on the back, congratulating ourselves for being fantastic. We have learned that self-deprecation and humility are admirable traits. And that they are. But they do not lead to self-reflection that, in turn, can grow to a strengths oriented mindset. Well, for a few minutes you are allowed. Apparently, Don Clifton used to hold out his hands at parties, when meeting new people, and simply ask: "What makes you special?"

Have a think about it. What does make *you* special?

The Advantages of Identifying Strengths

Armed with a unified vocabulary to describe what most people already know about themselves anyway, people who take the CSF or other similar assessments can reflect on how they naturally do things and consider souping up their processes in a strengths-oriented manner to achieve higher performance. Once we know our talents, we can combine them with learned skills and existing knowledge to create strengths and in a strengths-oriented environment we can work more regularly in flow (see Chapter 10), get the PFC switched on (see Chapter 5), charge productivity, and powered by dopamine, live and work with a smile on our faces.

Furthermore, knowledge of your strengths can help you to optimize time and energy previously wasted on managing weaknesses. Being introduced to the bee-glasses mindset is a great start toward working and living differently but in my experience, the real "aha moment" comes when folks take a strengths assessment test. It is then that reflection goes through the ceiling and plans are made for genuine change.

Taking such a test can also be a proverbial shot in the arm for (underperforming) teams whose members might have hitherto struggled to understand why their colleagues acted as they did. When we can openly discuss our strengths and talents with each other, we can build and develop happier, more productive, and healthier teams. More on this in Chapter 11.

What the Critics Say about Strengths Tests

Over the years I have heard critics of strengths tests express their doubts about their statistical validity. "It's just a bunch of questions—how can that transpose to identifying my talents? There are similar tests in Cosmopolitan magazine." Some share concerns about the accuracy or nature of the reports. "It is like reading a horoscope. Anyone could find bits in these texts that they could relate to themselves." And some articulate chagrin at the test procedure itself. I sometimes wanted to answer neither left nor right! The middle option seems to mean *don't know, don't care,* and *both*—how can that be?

Let's go through those one by one.

It's Just Like a Cosmo' Questionnaire!

They are, indeed, only questions. But until we have invented a machine which we can plug into people's heads to read their thoughts, such methodology is the closest we can get to helping people understand their motives, attitudes, and drivers. That said, I expect significant statistical sturdiness from such tests to help me learn about myself. I would not accept tests like we find in fitness magazines or on the Internet. (I once took two Star Wars tests on the same day. According to their results, I am most like Princess Leia *and* Jabba the Hutt.) So let us take a look at the statistical relevance of the above assessments. In the next couple of paragraphs, I do not want to lose anyone with a load of stodgy statistical terminology, but it is important to me that you are able to assess the validity—and so trustworthiness—of results from any of the above tests, or any which you may choose to take.

There are established indicators commonly used to assess whether a psychometric tool measures what it is actually supposed to. If we can find that it does just that, then we can regard it as being empirically and statistically valid. In other words, we can trust its results to help us realistically with our self-reflection. There are three ways of assessing test validity (Lopez & Snyder 2003):

Discriminant validity (DV) (Campbel & Fiske 1959) shows us whether the items that the test claims to be distinct are indeed different from one another. A test that claimed to show how strongly you score on eight defined personality traits, for example, would be ineffective if two of those traits were in fact so similar that they overlapped. DV is shown as a decimal out of a maximum of 1. Any test with a DV over 0.85 is considered to be poor or have no DV (Henseler 2015).

The second check of test reliability is internal consistency (IC). It assesses whether a question designed to ascertain a particular characteristic actually does. It would be not good at all, if questions 27 and 29 claimed to investigate your levels of natural dedication, for example, but didn't actually do so. A statistical mechanism known as Cronbach's alpha is used to calculate IC. Anything lower than 0.7 suggests that the questions are not querying what they assert to (McCrae et al. 2011).

And thirdly, when you take a psychometric test, you want it to represent a generalized picture of your personality and not just a snapshot of how you are feeling at one particular moment (Bland & Altman 1986).

If you take a test on Monday and then again a few weeks or months later, you would like the results to be similar. That would suggest to you that your traits and talents are recurring mannerisms and not just one-off thoughts. The same is true of other tests or experiments. If you measured yourself at 5 ft 7 in with a tape measure on Thursday and the same measuring tape showed that you were 6 ft 6 in the following Tuesday, then you would probably start to doubt the efficacy of the tape. The measuring tool should show stability in its results across time. A test–retest reliability score of 1.0 would represent perfect correlation between the two test results. Most statisticians agree that 0.7 upward suggests valid test reliability over time (Shuttleworth 2019).

Here are the DV, IC, and test–retest reliability scores (where available) for the four talent assessments covered in this chapter (Table 9.1). I'll let you make your own mind up as to their reliability.

Table 9.1 A Summary of the Statistical Reliability of Strengths Assessments

Assessment Type	Num- ber of Talents	Dis- criminant Validity	Internal Consis- tency	Test– Retest Reliability	Price
Clifton Strengths[6]	34	n/a	0.61	0.70	$19.99– $49.99
High 5[7]	20	0.29	0.87	0.81	Free– $29.99
strengthsprofile[8]	60	n/a	0.82	0.71	$14–$40
VIA-IS[9]	24	n/a	>0.70[10]	>0.80	Free–$20

The Reports Are Like a Horoscope!

All I would say to this one is read the reports from your last-placed talent themes. When you read about which talent themes you are least well versed in, I predict you will have a physiological aversion to them.

---

[6]Schreiner (2006).

[7]High5Test (2019). These are larger font than the footnotes below.

[8]https://strengthsprofile.com/en-gb/resources/technicalmanual.

[9]https://en.wikipedia.org/wiki/Values_in_Action_Inventory_of_Strengths#Validity_and_reliability

[10]Sadly more detailed statistics could not be found for this test.

When I think about what my life would be like, if I lived with those bottom five or six talents to the fore, then the hairs stand up on the back of my neck and my stomach starts turning over. I cannot possibly imagine working and communicating in such a manner. It would feel so foreign to me. Unnatural. Dare I say, wrong. Test results have shown in me, for example, that I show very little natural talent for deliberativeness. I have a talent for cracking on with it; getting things done and starting with gusto but I rarely take a moment to carefully consider which might be the right way or the safest way or whatever. There is no profile text in the world describing the talent of deliberation, which if I were to read it, would convince me that that is a natural yearning and talent of mine.

The profile texts are written in a positive bee-glasses style. No doubt about that. Presumably a crackerjack team of PR, marketing, and copywriter guys and girls have tweaked and tuned them to sound as inspirational as they do, but their nuts and bolts—i.e., the key messages they send—are collated absolutely scientifically and presented systematically using algorithms only a handful of people in the world are allowed to know. If you answer question 17 this way for example, question 88 that way, and question 92 another way, then the system will methodically piece your profile together so that it accurately reflects your individual version of that talent. No two profile texts are the same but remember it is not some holy set of commandments, anyway. They were not carved in stone and their reader does not have to adhere to them religiously. The words are meant to stimulate you to self-reflect, nothing more. They are the road map, not the road.

The Testing Procedure Confused Me!

This one is harder to swipe away with stats. OK, I will give you this one. Sitting, staring at a computer screen for anything up to 45 minutes, answering question after question—some of which may sound abstract or be concepts that one cannot immediately identify with—is not everyone's idea of the perfect night in. Some coachees have told me that when they took the test they found the process a bit repetitive; sometimes tedious.

Furthermore, some complained that the limited options of answer left, answer right, or neutral in the middle didn't allow them the nuanced answer they would have preferred to give. This can seem frustrating. The middle response represents "I do not know," "both," and "I do not care"—all of which are decidedly different basic positions. Once again, I will return to the argument I have made a couple of times: Such tests are just there to help you. Invest half an hour and it becomes a stimulus that motivates you to years of self-reflection and development. In my experience, the fox—in this case—is worth the chase.

Hide not your talents, they for use were made,
What's a sundial in the shade?

US Founding Father, Benjamin Franklin

CHAPTER 10

Leveraging Strengths and Dealing with Weaknesses

What Is Talent

You may have noticed that I have used both the words "strength" and "talent" interchangeably in this book up until now. Actually, that has been slightly disingenuous of me. When we are dealing with positive psychology and all things cognitive/professional performance, then they should be considered very distinct phenomena.

Talents, in this context, can be thought of as inherent or genetically inherited characteristics or mental patterns, which make it simpler for us to learn and complete certain cognitive tasks. Now, I do not want you to make any connection between the word "talent" within this frame of reference and its overuse in TV newcomer jury-singing shows or holiday camp open mic nights or at sports team trial days or anything of that nature. I do not want you to make the connotation with glitz or glamour, nor think of someone with cognitive talents as *special* or amazing or a *superstar*. I sat and shared a drink in Brussels, Belgium one day last year with a very gifted musician, I know. I told him that he had talents but before I could add that I thought he could further develop some of them into powerful strengths and that he could maybe learn some useful tips to help him leverage those strengths still further. He vociferously rebutted my initial claim that he had talent:

> I resent that. That sounds like all my success in life has just fallen out of the sky and landed on my lap. I am no more special than that guy over there. I have got to where I am today with hard work, dedication, and blood sweat and tears. Anyone could do what I do. It is unfair to suggest that I am only successful because I magically have *talent*!

That is the problem with the word talent. It is reminiscent of the beauty-pageant mom gushingly overpraising her "talented little super bunny" or the competitive soccer dad regaling his mates at the bar of his "amazingly talented son, who is attracting loads of attention from scouts." Forget that use of the word talent. That is not what we are talking about here. Talent does not make you special and it is certainly not a get-out-of-jail-free card nor is it a free ticket to the top. That is why I quickly wanted to find the right words in Belgium that day to better help my friend appreciate that. A better translation of "talent," which I consequently developed over my light, Belgium beer that day in Brussels would be:

> Talent = Accidental, naturally occurring, specific
> cognitive proclivity.

Pithy, I know.

Talent is *not* what mysteriously beamed you to where you are today without the need for any work or control on your part. Nor is it the proverbial "Advance to go-collect $200" card. It is merely a series of accidentally occurring, well-trodden synaptic pathways in your PFC. A few million gaps between a few million neurons. That's it. But what you can, potentially, do with those gaps….oh that can be very interesting indeed.

Think back to the above-average readers in Glock's speed-reading experiment (Chapter 6). They could rather unbelievably read 2,900 words per minute after training. But they could *not* read nearly as many before the training. Barely 10 percent as many. They could only read around 350 words per minute before training. They could not have achieved those 2,900 words per minute without a talent. Of that there is no doubt. But it is not the talent *alone* that got them there. That is obvious, because when Glock first tested them their performance was 880 percent weaker. If talent alone advanced us straight to "go" then we wouldn't have to learn or practice anything. What got them to that phenomenal level of achievement was not only talent, it was the *combination* of their "accidental, naturally occurring, specific cognitive proclivity" for reading fast (they could already read three times quicker than the average) combined with skills learned in the speed-reading training course.

Glock described the student with the best performance in the speed-reading challenges as: "interesting." He scored a 136 out of a possible 162—way above the sample average 105—in the Terman Group Test of Mental Ability—an IQ test taken by the subjects. He had an over-average school grade of 93 percent; significantly higher than the average 83 percent and Glock adds that the boy had shared with the testers that his mother had expressed an interest in him improving his reading. Glock also mentions that the boy had shown a highly competitive attitude during the testing phase by setting himself successive goals of 500, then 1,000, then 2,000 words per minute. Sadly, Glock is never specific about his intentions in sharing these qualitative, extraneous descriptions of the boy's academic performance and character but my assumption is that he is strongly suggesting that it was not talent alone that helped the boy reach top performance.

He benefited from three learning methods (over the period of about a month), he had the moral and emotional support of his mother, he showed drive and determination to continually improve, and he was academically one of the very best among his peers. It seems that our 2,900 word-per-minute genius had combined his natural talent for speed reading with the right skills, knowledge, and drive. This is what makes a strength.

For those of you with an accidental, naturally occurring, specific cognitive proclivity[1] for numbers and calculations, please look away now. This approach may offend you. I am aware that the following is not a real equation and that it probably does not adhere to universal mathematical laws. For the rest of you—here is how you make a strength. Strengths are what you get if you add **knowledge** to **skill**, multiply them with **drive**, and then leverage it all to the power of **talent**.

$$(\text{Skills} + \text{Knowledge}) \times \text{Drive}^{\text{Talent}} = \text{STRENGTHS}$$

You could be gifted with all the talent in the world but it alone will not get you anywhere near best-in-class performance. To achieve high performance you do, indeed, have to *start* with talent but then you also have to learn the relevant skills to help you solve that particular challenge,

---

[1] That is the last time I will call it that, I promise.

know the right subject knowledge to become an expert in that field, and pepper the whole dish with a healthy dollop of drive.

I could be born with a "gift of the gab." I could be one of those people who never needs to search for the right word. A natural-born rhetorician. The silkiest of persuasive skills. But that chat alone will not make me a world-class salesperson! To be a top key account executive and sell complex, valuable products to informed customers in a saturated market, I will need more than just good sales patter. Top sellers need to be right up to date with the current trends in their industry, in order to be able to answer tough questions from clients or to compare their product to other rival products. They also need to know where to find the niche target group for their particular wares. Which branch-specific exhibitions or fairs do those customers go to? Which federations are they members of? (Knowledge).

I could have a natural talent for public speaking. I am not afflicted by nerves disturbing my flow. I relish that buzz that I get back from an interested audience. I have a natural ability to communicate complex matters in a way that lay people can easily understand and I instinctively gesticulate in a stimulating and engaging way. But if I don't know how to use slideshow software such as PowerPoint© or Keynote© or Prezi©, then I will probably not excel in the modern business world. If my flipcharts and other written media look like I have scrawled them with the pen in my mouth, then my presentations will lack that professional finish. If I do not learn to support my voice, or to project loudly without damaging my throat, then my presentation invitations will dry out as quickly as my vocal chords (Skills).

Or I could have the (almost)complete package: Never-ending creativity, imagination, and zest for design (talent). The high-end techniques to get the very best out of all the cutting-edge media tools out there (skills). The phone numbers of all the top design agencies (knowledge). But I sadly lack the motivation and get-up-and-go to pick up the receiver and make that call. I'll get around to updating my website sometime. I will add my profile to that freelancer portal next week. In the meantime, I will doodle a masterpiece on this coffee shop napkin. All the talent, skills, and knowledge in the world but no drive. The mercurial ex-professional soccer player George Best had an abundance of natural talent. He had all the skills in the book. Many described him as one of the most naturally gifted players ever to have played the game (Warrington 2017). He also knew everything he needed to know about the sport but he famously retired twice at the tender age of 27. Uninjured but, seemingly, uninterested. After the electric beginning to his career, he was seldom again able to tune his skills into strengths. He, apparently, did not have the drive to do so. To live and work strengths oriented—and so reach peak performance—I need *all* the terms, variables, and operators of the (pseudo)equation above.

My guy in Belgium was right about almost everything. It is not his talent alone that got him to where he is now.[2] Yes, he was born with a spell-binding talent for music—he can hear multiple-part harmony in his head and can identify which instrument is out of tune in a 90-piece orchestra, for example. But he practiced his scales and arpeggios ad nauseam for hours and hours per day from the age of 3 to hone his musical ability. (*skills*). He learned to understand and use a language fluently. A language which is foreign to most of us: the language of crotchets, staves, octaves, quavers, and minims (*knowledge*). And, throughout his career, his passion and de-termination to make it in the music industry has also seen him do the hard graft to help make that (next) breakthrough. At the beginning of his career, he played piano on cruise ships, in bars and in run-down theaters in paro-chial European towns. That *drive*, combined with the other parameters in the strengths equation, has taken him to the London Palladium, the Royal Albert Hall, and to Abbey Road Studios. Not just talent alone.

However, I disagree with him still on one of his arguments. Anyone could *not* do what he does. Many could try and many have but without his talent, they will almost certainly never achieve his career heights. To prove this, take a look at the equation from a different perspective. I have repeat-edly stressed the value of talent but what would the result be if we took out the talent-lever? How high would you climb if you developed the right skills, learned the know-how you need in that field, and then worked very, very hard? (Taylor 2019). The answer is: Not to the (very) top.

The Eight Tips

Once we've recognized our talents, it is absolutely imperative that we nur-ture them and leverage them to ensure that they apex into strengths. At

---

[2] He is one of the most sought-after orchestral conductors in the world.

the same time, cultivating and enforcing certain life hacks to compensate for our weaknesses can also help us to vastly reduce wasted time and fruitless endeavor. These are resources which we can then reinvest into developing our strengths even further and achieving even more.

To this end, here they are: eight gems; consisting of pointers for how to leverage your strengths and of tactics for mitigating the negative impact of your weaknesses.

Leveraging Strengths

1. Transparently discuss your strengths and weakness and those of your process partners. Once you have identified and reflected upon your strengths and weaknesses, it is vital that those around you who work with or share time with you, are also aware. Such transparency will help your co-workers to better understand how—and in particular—*why* you do the things you do. This knowledge can, in turn, reduce the potential for conflict and lead to a much more harmonious working environment for all. My colleagues and I refer to each other's strengths all the time. "Why don't you take this project—it will require quick action to be taken and you have 'activator', so that will fit perfectly." "I've got 'deliberative' so I am happy to check the document for mistakes." "I have 'ideation' at 34 so someone else should probably sit on the think tank in my place." If your process partners and you all share each other's strengths with one another transparently, then it makes division of labor and delegation a simplicity.

2. Actively implement your talents in a strengths-oriented manner
    This one might sound glaringly obvious but it is amazing and sad in equal measure how many coachees of mine over the years have raved about the strengths-based approach when introduced to it, only to report back weeks later that they would "love to work on strengths more but just don't have the time." I'm afraid that is no excuse. Changing one's approach to work is a paradigm switch of mindset and, like any change process, requires time and attention. In addition, I hope that the irony of mundane time-thieves stealing so much of your precious energy that you have no time left over to dedicate to self-development and self-reflection is not lost on you.

Eighty percent of people feel that they don't get the chance to use their strengths at work (Matson & Robinson 2017) but only 17 percent of people do anything about it. If you want to develop your strengths more, you simply have to find the time to implement your talents. That means realigning how you complete tasks to spend more of your time using your talents and strengths.

3. Reflect on your strengths further with a qualified strengths coach

I cannot recommend enough; spending time reflecting on your strengths together with a strengths coach. Having a list of new terms in front of you, having to understand what they all mean, learning to identify the signs of different talents, and having to read pages and pages of accompanying explanations and case studies can be extremely daunting and time-consuming.

A strengths coach can help you to quickly get an overview of your talents and to recognize, understand, and reflect in the right way. Some coaches will work with pictures or cartoons or cards to help stimulate your appreciation of the model. Others might ask many systemic questions to nudge you toward the calm and excitement that comes from knowing what you are really, really good at. Regardless of the technique they use, find one whom you feel comfortable working with. A handful of sessions should be more than enough for a strengths coach worth her weight in salt to point you in the right direction.

4. Training and personal development

As we saw from Glock's work (1955), training works. If you feel that you are poor at presenting, then sign yourself up for a presentation skills workshop. The facilitator can school you in the art of vocal projection, dealing with nerves, using different media to support your message, learning the shortcuts in slideshow software, structuring your logic, and dealing with questions from the audience, etc. If you are the kind of presenter who stands in front of their audience, face hidden behind your A4 notes, hands shaking wildly, voice breaking like a pubescent teenager, reading verbatim from slide after slide of jam-packed unattractive, overly long bullet points, then that kind of workshop could be for you.

But you should attend the training course with a clear head and fitting expectations. You will almost certainly not miraculously leave the course with the silky oratory skills of a Barack Obama, nor will you suddenly find yourself creating eye-catching visuals which look better suited on a huge screen at a Wembley Stadium rock concert than in a dark board room. Training and other personal development measures (such as coaching, mentoring, shadowing, etc.) can lead to improvement but if you want absolute, high performance then—as you well know by now—you have to start with talent.

Managing Weaknesses

5. Build up and employ complementary partnerships

If your colleagues and you were aware of what you can all do well, just think of how you could start the discussion about who does what. Instead of ineffectively slogging through the same old tasks, you could divide up responsibilities and assign tasks to those who want them and can perform them at their best. This approach to delegating according to strengths is deeply human (see Chapter 4) and can be traced back to how our ancestors shared out tasks and responsibilities among themselves, based on their proclivities, to solve their clan's problems.

Most of us are instinctively aware of the possibilities of building complementary partnerships. If you needed your satellite dish repaired but had no electrical or digital communications expertise, you would ask your friend the engineer to help. In return, you would spend a few hours working in her garden as you have a joy for flowers and a gift for creating beautiful, colorful flower beds. The same is true at work, of course. Asking a colleague with a talent for graphic design to format my slideshow for me, while I check for errors in their document (e.g., I have always found proofreading easy and exciting) is totally logical and would save us both time and energy and ensure that both tasks are performed competently.

I engage the services of a professional accountant to complete my tax returns for me.

I *could* feasibly do it myself. I know how to read the forms and instructions from the tax administration.

I *could* collate all relevant receipts and invoices and correlate them with the respective transactions.

I *could* even go through every slip and enter its amount into the corresponding account and then calculate my tax burden and send all the correct documents off to the Inland Revenue.

But I choose not to. I have long since realized that I do not have the natural talents best suited for high-quality completion of the above tasks. I don't have the organizational skills required for filing and documenting all the hundreds of bills. I have neither the patience nor attention to detail to input all of the correct data into the correct cell without making a number of mistakes and I have never shown a flair for arithmetic, so calculating how much tax I should declare would not only be very challenging for me, it could potentially lead to serious issues down the line. Instead, as I mentioned, I employ the services of a gifted accountant, who kindly and apparently effortlessly processes every part of my tax declaration and meets every deadline on my behalf.

In a moment of pure strengths orientation, my tax advisor contacted me recently and asked for me to coach her for a presentation that she was asked to deliver at a conference. We both have talents in our respective fields and we have developed a complimentary partnership to help each other work far more productively.

6. Establish support systems

If we think of complimentary partnerships as the human strengths balancing act, then establishing support systems is its mechanical cousin. If you do not have strengths in certain areas, then you should try to mitigate your blind spots with machines, processes, and tools or the like. I mentioned the dreaded tax declaration—if there was a CliftonStrengths talent theme for "collating-documentation-required-for-the-tax-declaration," then I would probably have it at 35.[3] I have always found it very taxing.[4] I tire easily and quickly of looking at large amounts of numbers. I find it hard to recognize patterns in complex

---

[3] The Gallup list only goes up to 34.
[4] Pun intended.

numerical collections and my instinct is not to check data deliberately nor complete such tasks in a disciplined manner. All not ideal, because as a freelance facilitator, I have a legal requirement to submit mistake-free income and expenditure documentation to the federal tax authority every month. I have an acceptable standard which must be met and so there is no possibility for me to avoid it. I have to complete my tax declaration and I have to do it right.

I did always do so but it cost me enormous amounts of energy. Deeply rooted in Limbic System and with cortisol doing its dastardly work, I *wasted* at least a day month fishing seemingly endless receipts out of my shoebox labeled "TAX" before begrudgingly cross-checking them against the transactions on the bank statement. I had to force myself to barely achieve acceptable standard but I hated every second. But I have been saved[5] by establishing support systems. For the last nearly 2 years, I have had technology complete my P&L for me. I use an online service which automatically draws down all my invoices from providers like Internet, phone, and insurance companies and then automatically sends them to another app I have, which robotically connects the correct bill with the right transaction. A cell phone app, which scans in the remaining paper receipts and automatically files them with the correct expenditure completes my dream package of support systems. They mitigate my weaknesses, allowing me to free-up considerably more time on leveraging my strengths. Support systems do not have to be of the digital variety as per my example but they can be a very powerful tool in strengths orientation.

7. Just do it! (aka the Nike™ approach)

Not having a talent in a particular area is no excuse to not get stuck in. You cannot say: "Well, I don't have the talent 'communication', so I'm just not going to answer the phone at work!" Nor can you think "I don't have analytical talents so I'm just not going to check this spreadsheet." That attitude is unacceptable, I'm afraid. Even if you don't want to—you have a responsibility to come into the office wearing pants. "I don't have a talent for identifying fashion trends so I'm gonna come to work in my boxer shorts!" Nope. Not ok.

---

[5]Slightly more tenuous pun intended.

Even if you are not great at everything; even if you get no buzz from it and rarely get into flow, you still have to knuckle down and get *certain* things done. Sure, you probably won't achieve top performance in those areas. Sure, you may not like doing them, but if they are requirements of your role, then you just have to crack on with them. A nice mnemonic here is the slogan used by the sports company Nike. It may not turn out perfect, but: Just do it.

8. As a last resort, find the position that suits the strengths

And last but by no means least. If the struggling employee and his or her supervisor have intensively attempted tips 1 to 7 over a period of *several months* but still little or no improvement in productivity and well-being is observed, then maybe he or she is in the wrong role. There is, as the proverb goes, no point in flogging a dead horse. If my colleague shows neither talent nor interest in a particular task or tasks and the above interventions have not changed the status quo, then maybe it is time to cut ties to allow all concerned to find themselves more fitting responsibilities.

If leveraging other strengths and managing weaknesses as suggested above has not worked and the process partner is still not getting out of first gear, expending huge energy to achieve the same results others achieve with ease, or is dissatisfied at work, then it is time for all parties concerned to be adult and professional and cut ties. That is not to say that I suggest you go around wildly firing people the moment that they do not exhibit obvious strength in a particular task. Developing strengths is a nuanced challenge that requires patience and diligence from all parties. Give people time. Work with them. Transparently discuss their development over weeks and months and work together to develop their strengths and cover their weaknesses, where possible. But when enough is enough, then do the right thing and try to help your colleague find a position where they can blossom with their strengths. We all know someone who was miserable in their role then one day jacked it all in and did something completely different and is now loving life; in the zone. That someone could be your colleague who is currently struggling to find their feet.

Talent wins games, but teamwork and intelligence win championships.

Ex-professional basketballer, Michael Jordan

CHAPTER 11

Identifying Strengths in Others

Up until now in this book, we have looked mainly introspectively. But we do not operate in a bubble. The vast majority of the world's productivity stems from collaboration and it is a truism that "teams perform best when the team itself has a balanced, complementary set of strengths" (Rath & Conchie 2008). So to achieve high performance, it is just as essential to recognize and leverage the strengths of those around us as it is to grapple with our own. So which are the best strengths, then? Which talents and strengths will take the leader and his team the farthest? Would it be best to have loads of rhetorical wizards in the team to charm and persuade their clients into purchases? Or would a team full of precise auditors be best to make sure not a bean slips through the books? Or does the perfect team need activators and catalysts with drive to take the initiative in choppy waters? The answer is, of course, not for the first time, that many roads lead to Rome. There is certainly *no* perfect leader and by the same token there is *no* quintessential mix of talents that represents the perfect manager's strengths profile. Just take a cursory look at the world of politics or at sports coaches or captains and you will see how diverse leaders can be. What is more, the perfect member of staff's strengths profile is also a myth.

It's All about the Mix

The perfect team member does not exist. However, having a mix of strengths prevalent *across* all team's members is vital (Gladis 2008). If a manager surrounded herself with like-minded, like-talented clones, then the results would be predictable: Challenges in certain areas would be quickly and effortlessly solved, while others may receive little attention as the whole team shows neither the willingness nor the aptitude to engage. The perfect team needs a delicious and diverse mix of talents just as a dish would taste pretty bland if its cook only poured in one ingredient.

Before we address how to go about establishing that perfectly strengths-balanced team, let us first reflect on how leaders traditionally build their teams. Invariably one of three typical approaches is used.

- The gut-feeling approach
  I have lost count of the amount of leaders who have told me over the years that they apply no system whatsoever to assembling teams. Instead they rely solely on their instinct. "If I get a good feeling about someone, when I meet them, then I hire them there and then; on the spot!" a coachee of mine told me recently. (He is the MD of a Europe-wide business entity and manages 400 people.) I am not aware of a study that has yet proved the existence of a magical personality-identification superpower but it is incredible how many leaders claim to have just such a skill. Most of us are not FBI profilers and even if we were, we shouldn't be making the monumentally naïve assumption that we can read people's strengths and weaknesses, in myriad, complex pressure situations after having shared a coffee with them. A sports coach would never dream of putting a new player in the lineup without having seen him or her perform at least a number of times in trial games or in training. A choreographer would rather cancel the show than throw a would-be ballerina on stage without knowing—in detail—what her dancing skills are and a conductor would not dream of bringing a musician into their orchestra without having heard them play a number of different pieces. So why do business managers and team leaders continue to insist on putting their teams together without the faintest notion of their members' strengths?

- The CV approach
  Admittedly, slightly more scientific than the telepathic superheroes from the gut-feeling approach but even this age-old technique for identifying talent has its own inherent weaknesses. CVs (and cover letters and online profiles on job sites) can be notoriously doctored

to look more appealing and references offered are all too rarely contacted. Even if they are, such enquiry can easily become a subjective case of "he said, she said." If a previous boss had a bad experience with your applicant or clashed with them personally, then it is unlikely that they will provide a glowing reference. Even if they do, it is hard for you to appreciate whether their experience will match yours as your organization's environments and cultures are likely very distinct. Even if CV entries *are* entirely accurate *and* references completely positive and honest, the contents of such documents still cannot provide a team-building leader with the information they need to form a strengths-based team. Lest we forget the hilariously banal attempts by applicants to cover all the bases by including statements in their cover letters such as "I am comfortable working as part of a team but also enjoy working independently." In fact, the more entertaining thing is that organizations employ people based on such abstract, vague self-assessment and self-marketing. The degree qualification gained, the title of the dissertation written, the budgets handled, the industries worked in, the companies worked for do not describe *how* the applicant works. They may describe the knowledge or experience they have (i.e., the what) but their methods (the how) can only be appreciated by recognizing people's strengths.

- The Peter Principle

  The Peter Principle is a theory posited by Laurence J. Peter in 1969 (Lazear 2000), which describes the all-too-common phenomenon of continuous promotion until failure kicks in. According to Peter, we have traditionally promoted those who are most successful in their role to take on a new role, and we do that until they have been boosted to a position to which they are not actually suited, and so fail, and are, inevitably, fired. Put another way, we all have talents and strengths, and it is the expression of these strengths that catch our superiors' eyes and sometimes lead to our promotion. However, it is very possible that we had the strengths in *that* role to catch the eye, but that by no means guarantees that we have the strengths to be successful in the *next* role. Just because I am the best in my field or the best in my team does not mean that I will necessarily be the best at *leading* that team.

All of these approaches have their merits but none of them rewards genuine, relevant, excellence. None of them focuses on strengths. Great leaders populate and lead their teams according to its inherent members' strengths—not based on their resumes, reputation, or qualifications. Building teams according to their members' strengths can ensure that all blind spots are filled, and that all team members have the best chance of reaching their full potential for and as part of the team.

Probably one of the best treatises on the makeup of strengths-based teams is "Strengths Based Leadership" by Barry Conchie and Tom Rath. They took a close look at what constitutes a successful team and presented essential tips for the leader looking to build his or her team according to strengths. In researching their 2009 book, they drew upon an unprecedented depth of data taken from 20,000 in-depth interviews with senior leaders, 10,000 discussions with followers, analysis of over 1 million work teams, and facts and figures relevant to strengths-based collaboration extracted from 50 years of polling data.

Their first finding from that mega dataset, right off the bat, was a humdinger: *The best leaders invest in their people's strengths.*

You may not be surprised to read such a sentence in a book about strengths orientation but its influence is undeniable based on the research sample size. I will write it again because its ramifications are so important.

The most successful leaders (based on over 1 million analyzed teams) focus on their employees' strengths.

However, as we know, so many leaders choose not to, preferring instead to dangle carrots, threaten with sticks, or focus on processes. Indeed, only a third of Americans claim to be able to use their strengths at work every day. That is a dismal waste of potential and I place the blame firmly at the door of our leaders. Leaders should recognize their process partners' strengths and afford the opportunity for them to be used in a strength-based environment. But how do leaders do that if they do not have access to a strengths assessment (see Chapter 9)?

Signs of Talent

If managers don't have the possibility to put their teams through a strengths assessment or to send them to a strengths workshop, there are two easy yet powerful first steps toward identifying strengths in others. The first is to observe your colleagues in their working environment. Gallup identifies five typical indicators which, when spotted, highly likely point back to a naturally occurring talent.

Desire

People usually have a natural yearning toward activities where they have a chance to exercise their talents. If people around us are working in a certain way then we, instinctively, either feel drawn toward their style or not. If we feel that draw then, chances are, there is a talent behind that craving. When responsibilities are delegated, those who speak up and express interest in particular tasks are probably doing so because they feel a natural yearning toward that way of working. That is probably based on experience of successes in the past. It may well be the result of synaptic paths well-trodden in the brain. When we pine for a certain way of working, it is almost certainly linked back to our talents.

Rapid Learning

Has anyone ever shown you something and you picked it up, almost immediately? Have you ever watched a how-to video on the Internet and found yourself completing the challenge even before the vlogger has finished teaching you? Or can you remember explaining certain academic concepts to fellow students at school or at college, unable to remember when and where you learned it yourself? You just kind of "got" it and it went right in and stayed in. Rapid and effortless learning is a key indicator that talent and strengths are at play.

Flow

Have you ever been driving, your mind wandering from this subject to that, when you catch yourself and realize that you cannot remember any part of your journey from the last minutes. "Have I already left the city? I don't remember passing through the forest." Your mind has been able to decompartmentalize and focus on certain subjects and pay less obvious attention, for those minutes, to the action of driving. You are in flow.

Your experience of and gift for driving allows your brain to automate its mechanisms to free up cognition for other matters. When you ask yourself "wow, where did the time go?" or you struggle to recall how you got to now, you are in the zone, working with your talents. You don't have to think about what you are doing—it just seems to be happening on its own accord. Do you remember our friend Mihaly Csikszentmihalyi way back in Chapter 1? It was he who first coined the term flow after some of his interviewees described the feeling of immersion in energized focus as being reminiscent of floating effortlessly down a river. He had previously called it autotelic personality (from Greek: auto meaning *self* and telic meaning *goal*). I can see why he changed it to flow.

Nakamura and Csikszentmihalyi (2009) identify six factors as signs that a person is in a state of flow:

- Intense and focused concentration on the here and now
- A joining of awareness and action
- A loss of self-reflection
- A sense of personal control over the situation
- A distortion of temporal experience, time can seem to fly or stand still
- A feeling of great intrinsic reward (see Chapter 8)

Being in flow is a powerful sign that you are working with your strengths.

Glimpses of Excellence

Whereas being in flow is akin to the feeling: how did I get here? The glimpse of excellence prompts you to ask yourself the question: how did I do that? We have all experienced moments in our life where we have achieved greatness (no matter how small the accomplishment) and when others have asked, "how did you do that" you counter with some unsubstantial response like "Dunno. I just kinda did it!" Hello Mrs. Strength, you are very welcome. Ask your people how they achieved what they achieved. Help them to reflect on and be proud of how they completed complex tasks or solved seemingly insoluble problems—Mrs. Strength almost certainly had a hand in it.

Satisfaction

And last but not least—do what you enjoy and enjoy what you do. If you love your activities you will excel at them and if you excel at something you will love doing it. Reflect on your work for a minute. Which activities gave you a kick, either while you were working on them or, indeed, shortly after you finished them? Think back to when you asked yourself: "When can I do that again?" Working with our talents switches the PFC on in reward mode (see Chapter 5), gets the dopamine flowing, and it just makes us feel great. Delivering high performance is a buzz. If you did well at college recall that feeling when you got your exam results and looked down at that gleaming A grade, seemingly smiling back at you. Unbridled joy. Or maybe you have experienced that warming, content sensation as you leave your workplace after a triumphant day. You take a deep breath and soak up what it feels like to have been excellent—even if it was just for a little while. Watch the face of the elite sportsperson closely as she breaks that record or scores that goal. That satisfaction is the sweet, sweet taste of talent in action.

If you are a leader, take time out of your schedule to observe your delegates. Watch them and try to capture when they are in the zone (flow), learn rapidly, or enjoy glimpses of excellence. But don't stop there. Enter into transparent discussion with them about their strengths. Invite them for a hot drink and quiz them about those occasions when they worked with their talents. Don't give them the Spanish inquisition. Begin the conversation by sharing your interest for talent and tell them that you are interested in *their* strengths. Then ask them about what they desire to do, when they learn quickly, when they are in flow, when they glimpse excellence, and when they feel satisfaction. The reflection and knowledge will improve your respective collaboration markedly.

The Characteristics of Successful Teams

So we leaders have now done everything we can toward building a strengths-based team. We have constructed our team based on their talents. We have learned to identify moments of strength-fueled excellence and we are developing a culture of transparent, open self-reflection and strengths-oriented development. But how do we recognize if all that has worked or not? How do we discern whether our group is a top team?

When comparing observations from one million teams, and after cross-referencing them against the responses from interviews with over 30,000 leaders and followers, Rath and Conchie (2009) noticed clear, repeating patterns in top teams.

Result Orientation

Good teams don't get bogged down with conflicts and gossip. Good teams focus on results and work together to achieve those results. Strong teams may well have the odd argument toward attaining those goals but they don't let those disagreements cloud their ambitions. They keep discussions constructive and objective and don't hold grudges, construe statements as personal, or let perceived wrongs muddy their relationships. Successful business units have found ways to keep their collaborative focus oriented on results and not on one-upmanship or on interpersonal squabbles. Conflicts don't break up good teams. They are learned from, solved amicably, and not allowed to fester or poison teamwork from the inside.

Superior Target

Being focused on a shared goal is all well and good but if that goal is un-identified or not vocalized, then teams will suffer. Successful teams determine quickly what is best for their group and the organization and then prioritize efforts to achieve those goals. Strong teams see the big picture by identifying what is essential for the organization and then subordinating their own goals in favor of the greater good. Conchie and Rath note that this is not easy and requires dedication and a powerful belief in and respect for the brand but when it clicks it can be a potent dynamic. Great crews align on their commitment to their organization's goals and collectively develop processes and implement measures to that end.

Commitment

One of the subjects that I discuss most often with leaders, executives, and professionals is that of work–life balance. If I had a dollar for every time a coachee or workshop participant had told me that they have little time for hobbies or family because they are so dedicated to their jobs, then I would probably have enough money to take a few months out and … write them a time management book. Overwork and workaholism are the proverbial work–life cancers of our age. They have negative social and emotional repercussions (Spence & Robbins 1992), and have all sorts of health consequences (Sussman 2012). People who focus only on their work have been found to struggle to function effectively in their role, experience more frequent pain (McMillan & O'Driscoll 2004), and show a significantly greater chance of suffering from depression and back pain, and take more sick days due to mental health problems than those who balance the personal and professional lives (Matsudaira et al. 2013). But the most extraordinary fact pertaining to workaholism is that it doesn't even work. Overworking does not lead to more productivity. The best teams' members don't focus only on work; they are as committed to their personal lives as they are to their professional lives. They do not obsess over work. Strong teams spend quality time with their friends and families, commit to varied hobbies, and contribute to their communities through voluntary work and the like.

A coachee of mine once said: "It's ok. I'm in the rush-hour of my life. I'll slow down later." Not only may he never get the chance to slow down because of illness or burnout, but he will not even be reaching his full potential *during* his so-called "rush-hour."

Diversity

Strong teams embrace diversity. Period. Research has shown that the more diverse the group is with regard to age, gender, ethnicity, and (of course) talent, the more successful it will be. What is more, this should come as no surprise, as we as a species have had 2.6 million years of training to become successful together through diversity (see Chapter 4).

Attraction

Where do all the top graduates go? Teaching? Civil service? Retail? (Foote 2019). Nope. The top candidates are drawn toward other top co-workers.

Talent attracts talent. The highest performers want to work with other high performers. Put another way, great teams attract talent toward them. According to Hansen (2019), companies like Google, Microsoft, Apple, SAP, Facebook, Spotify, and Sky are red hot for attracting the best applicants and that is because such talent wants to work in great teams. Furthermore the same is true of internal applicants. If a job in the super-team is up for grabs within your organization, then you can bet your bottom dollar that HR will be peppered with transfer requests from superstars from other departments hoping to be a part of the dream team. In comparison, "weak teams start looking like abandoned tenements as people flee to a better place" (Gladis 2008).

My weaknesses... I wish I could come up with something. I'd probably have the same pause if you asked me what my strengths are. Maybe they're the same thing."

Actor, Al Pacino

Epilogue

Flipside of My Talents

I had intended the book to end here, but there is one more subject that, in all honesty, I have gone backward and forward in my mind about for ages as to whether I should even include it or not. Why the uncertainty? Well, because this final topic is, philosophically speaking, a huge leap from the rest of this work. I have, for 11 chapters, been on at you—with no little vociferation—about the importance of a positive, bee-glasses approach to work. Focus on the affirmative, I have said. Search out for talent, acknowledge it, and give it a space, I pleaded. Don't waste time on weaknesses, I argued—they will never morph into strengths, anyway. This polestar remains true and of huge importance, but it would be remiss of me if I were not to, at least, make you aware of this one last fly-glasses phenomenon. To truly make that mindset switch (Chapter 7) you deserve all the facts—and that includes the following dose of realism. As stunning as strengths orientation is, there exists a peculiarity which occurs under certain conditions, which you should keep an eye on.

When we exaggerate our strengths, they can, surprisingly easily, become our weaknesses. Although this paradox appears illogical at first glance, when placed under some investigation it starts to ring true.

Think all the way back to Chapter 2 where we discussed perception. Our actions are being permanently noticed or observed by others, and those others will generate their own, personal perception of what they see and hear. We have very little control over how we are perceived. Simply because it is not we who are doing the perceiving. Those watching you are using their own PFC and their own talents and strengths to filter what they experience. Now assume, for example, that your strengths set is mightily different from your observer's. What he or she sees will probably not naturally sit well with them. Your actions won't seem normal to them. "Why is she acting like that?," they may ask themselves. We all experience what we consider our own normal and that originates from our strengths. We instinctively approach certain challenges (including observations) in certain ways, and we do this because we have had success working like that in the past (knowledge), because we have learned the requisite abilities (skills), and (mainly) because we have certain naturally occurring proclivities (talents—see Chapter 10 for a refresh on these concepts). However what feels normal for us will not feel normal for others. Each of us has her own "normal."

OK. Fair enough. If we all recognize our difference, engage with others with respect, and accept that we all have (different) strengths to offer, then we should all get along swimmingly. Right? Yes. However there is only so much "abnormality" that we can take. When the actions we observe in others are overemphasized, then, after a point, it all becomes too much for us. Our brains enter threat mode, cortisol is released, the rationality in the PFC is inhibited, and we prepare ourselves to 'survive' the onslaught from this strangeness. In other words, when people overdo their talents, then their performance can appear so far from normal to others that it resembles eccentricity. You thought you were leveraging your strengths and were expecting high performance but—because you overstepped the mark—you have been shunned or are now embroiled in conflict.

We call this phenomenon "the flipside of your talents." Our talents are our Dr. Jekyll but, when we overplay them, we can quickly turn into Mr. Hyde. We need to recognize and utilize our strengths but we must have a keen sense of when too much is too much. I might have a wonderful natural talent for communication but if I let it run away with itself so much that it reveals its flipside, i.e., if I talk and talk and talk and talk, then some around me are very quickly going to revert to limbic system and the walls will go up. "Who is this guy? Why does he always go on and on? Why doesn't he let us get a word in edgeways? There's no point meeting with him—he never gives me a chance to contribute, anyway."

Or maybe I have strengths in deliberative, precise work. I am exact in my workings and that can be invaluable for my team and the organization's bottom line, but if I let my talent for deliberation spiral into pedantry, then I might very quickly alienate colleagues. We need to be as aware of the flipsides of our talents as we are the talents themselves. That is because flipsides don't only hurt those around us; they can, when left unchecked, hurt us too.

Take Pete for example. Pete has a talent for context. He looks back and learns from actions past. He reflects on his experiences and uses his learnings to adapt his attitude and performance accordingly. Sounds great. Useful talent. Progressive. Go Pete. But what if Pete overdoes his talent for context? What if he reflects and reflects and reflects, and—unable to abate the context/reflection machine in his head—cannot switch off and relax? I have worked with a number of coachees in the past who, unable to temper their talent for context, have experienced horrible bouts of insomnia, or have even suffered from depression or anxiety as a result of their Mr-Hyde-esque overexaggeration of their talent for context. The context/reflection machine in their heads runs over every experience ad nauseam not allowing them to slow down or even postpone reflection.

I could go through each talent and highlight their potential flipsides one by one but, frankly, each one of you will experience your talents differently and so, by definition, may exhibit altered flipsides. Keep those bee glasses on but, from time to time, take a moment to think about what happens to you and those around you if and when you lose control of your talent-wild-horse. Get regular feedback from trusted process partners on how and when they perceive your talents as flipsides and develop strategies to assuage Mr. Hyde.

Final Thoughts

Ok so that really is it, now. I couldn't possibly finish a book called "Strengths Orientation: The World Through Bee Glasses" on a negative note though so, for one last time, my two-pennies-worth.

Everyone reading this book has talents. Each one of you has the ability to deliver high performance in some field or fields and all of you have the right to work in PFC and be intrinsically motivated to want to achieve something and enjoy what you are doing. Whatever that may be. You do not have to slog through your work disengaged. You are allowed to search for an environment where you can actively use your strengths. You are not great at everything. You cannot all get whatever you want but you *can* be happy doing what you excel at. Find out about your talents. Take one of the tests mentioned in Chapter 9. Get some feedback from your peers and loved ones on what they notice about you and how you work or simply take some time to reflect on what you enjoy and where your strengths may lie (see Chapter 11).

I am often asked if there was one defining moment, when a metaphorical switch was flicked; leading me to suddenly embrace strengths orientation. The answer is no. There was no one "zero hour." My appreciation of the efficacy of positive psychology and of strengths-based leadership and collaboration took time. Apologies in advance for my use of this next, overused social science word but it was a *journey*. I experienced a whole lot of skepticism in me when I began to learn about this new paradigm. "What a load of pseudo-scientific, self-help mumbo-jumbo!" I began. However, slowly but ever so surely, as I uncovered more and more research, spoke to more and more professionals about their paradigmatic shift in experience, and as I learned of more and more success stories from practice, the pennies started to drop:

We have a limited time with each other on this planet.

We are spectacularly different from one another.

We are allowed to enjoy what we do.

We are good at some things.

We can be great at some things.

Our jagged diversity is our greatest strength.

I, for one, am not going to spend my remaining years searching for shit with my fly glasses on. I am going to search for the color and talent like a bee.

I'll leave you with the same words that my favorite singer songwriter Billy Joel ends every one of his gigs:

Don't take any shit from anyone!

Matt L. Beadle

February 2020

References

Adamson, R.E. 1952. "Functional Fixedness as Related to Problem Solving: A Repetition of Three Experiments." *Journal of Experimental Psychology* 44, no. 4, p. 288.

Alderfer, C.P. 1969. "An Empirical Test of a New Theory of Human Needs." *Organizational Behavior and Human Performance* 4, no. 2, pp. 142–75.

Amabile, T.M. 1996. *Creativity in Context: Update to the Social Psychology of Creativity*. London, England: Hachette.

Ariely, D. 2008 "What's the Value of a Big Bonus?" *New York Times.* https://nytimes.com/2008/11/20/opinion/20ariely.html, (accessed June 9, 2018).

Ariely, D., G. Loewenstein, and D. Prelec. 2006. "Tom Sawyer and the Construction of Value." *Journal of Economic Behavior & Organization* 60, no. 1, pp. 1–10.

Ariely, D., U. Gneezy, G. Loewenstein, and N. Mazar. 2009. "Large Stakes and Big Mistakes." *The Review of Economic Studies* 76, no. 2, pp. 451–69.

Asplund, J., J.K. Harter, S. Agrawal, and S.K. Plowman. 2016. "The Relationship Between Strengths-Based Employee Development and Organizational Outcomes 2015 Strengths Meta-Analysis," *Gallup 2015 Strengths Meta-Analysis Report.* https://static1.squarespace .com/static/577a17d9d482e9e2bce9bc68/t/58d4e81a20099e1b03 7cbced/1490348060515/2015+Relationship+between+Strengths-based+employee+development+and+organizational+outcomes+- +Gallup+StrengthsFinder+Singapore.pdf, (accessed March 4, 2020).

Bakker, A.B., and P.L. Costa. 2014. "Chronic Job Burnout and Daily Functioning: A Theoretical Analysis." *Burnout Research* 1, no. 3, pp. 112–19.

Beilock, S. 2010. *Choke: What the Secrets of the Brain Reveal about Getting It Right When You Have to*. New York, NY: Simon and Schuster.

Bland, J.M., and D.G. Altman. 1986. "Statistical Methods for Assessing Agreement between Two Methods of Clinical Measurement." *The Lancet* 327, no. 8476, pp. 307–10.

Bouchard, T.J., D.T. Lykken, M. McGue, N.L. Segal, and A. Tellegen. 1990. "Sources of Human Psychological Differences: The Minnesota Study of Twins Reared Apart." *Science* 250, no. 4978, pp. 223–28.

Brainy Quote. n.d. "Strengths Quotes." https://www.brainyquote.com/topics/strengths-quotes_2, (accessed March 4, 2020).

Brown, D.F., and D.D. Brown. 2003. *USMLE Step 1 Secrets: Questions You Will Be Asked on USMLE Step 1*. Philadelphia, PA: Belfus.

Campbell, D.T., and D.W. Fiske. 1959. "Convergent and Discriminant Validation by the Multitrait-Multimethod Matrix." *Psychological Bulletin* 56, pp. 81–105.

Chyun, Y.S., B.E. Kream, and L.G. Raisz. 1984. "Cortisol Decreases Bone Formation by Inhibiting Periosteal Cell Proliferation." *Endocrinology* 114, no. 2, pp. 477–80.

Cohen, P.A., J.A. Kulik, and C.-L.C. Kulik. 1982. "Educational Outcomes of Tutoring: A Meta-analysis of Findings." *American Educational Research Journal* 19, no. 2, pp. 237–48.

Corcoran, B. 2017. "Ever Feel Just 'Average'? Think Again, Says Todd Rose". https://www.edsurge.com/news/2017-06-12-ever-feel-just-average-think-again-says-todd-rose, (accessed March 4, 2020).

Cotton, P., and P.M. Hart. 2003. "Occupational Wellbeing and Performance: A Review of Organisational Health Research." *Australian Psychologist* 38, no. 2, pp. 118–27.

Crabb, S. 2011. "The Use of Coaching Principles to Foster Employee Engagement." *The Coaching Psychologist* 7, no. 1, pp. 27–34.

de Groot, J.H.B., M.A.M. Smeets, A. Kaldewaij, M.J.A. Duijndam, and G.R. Semin. 2012. "Chemosignals Communicate Human Emotions." *Psychological Science* 23, no. 11, pp. 1417–24.

de Quervain, D.J.-F., B. Roozendaal, and J.L. McGaugh. 1998. "Stress and Glucocorticoids Impair Retrieval of Long-Term Spatial Memory." *Nature* 394, pp. 787–90.

Drucker, P.F. 2006. *Classic Drucker: Essential Wisdom of Peter Drucker from the Pages of Harvard Business Review*. Boston, MA: Harvard Business Press.

Dubreuil, P., J. Forest, and F. Courcy. 2014. "From Strengths Use to Work Performance: The Role of Harmonious Passion, Subjective Vitality, and Concentration." *The Journal of Positive Psychology* 9, no. 4, pp. 335–49.

Duncker, K., and L.S. Lees. 1945. "On Problem-solving." *Psychological Monographs* 58, no. 5, p. i.

Durben Local History Museums. 2018. "Mrs Ples (Or Is It Mr Ples?)" https://durbanhistorymuseums.org.za/mrs-ples-or-is-it-mr-ples/, (accessed March 4, 2020).

Ebrecht, M., J. Hextall, L.-G. Kirtley, A.Taylor, M. Dyson, and J. Weinman. "Perceived Stress and Cortisol Levels Predict Speed of Wound Healing in Healthy Male Adults." *Psychoneuroendocrinology* 29, no. 6, pp. 798–809.

Eisenhower, R., and L. Shanock. 2003. "Rewards, Intrinsic Motivation, and Creativity: A Case Study of Conceptual and Methodological Isolation." *Creativity Research Journal* 15, nos. 2–3, pp. 121–30.

Fabritius, F., and H.W. Hagemann. 2018. *The Leading Brain: Powerful Science-Based Strategies for Achieving Peak Performance.* London, England: Penguin.

Flagel, S.B., J.J. Clark, T.E. Robinson, L. Mayo, A. Czuj, I. Willuhn, C.A. Akers, S.M. Clinton, P.E. M. Phillips, and H. Akil. 2011. "A Selective Role for Dopamine in Stimulus–Reward Learning." *Nature* 469, no. 7328, pp. 53–57.

Foote, A. 2019. "Where Do College Graduates Go For Jobs?" https://www.census.gov/library/stories/2019/08/where-do-college-graduates-go-for-jobs.html, (accessed March 4, 2020).

Freeburg, N. 2014. "What Is the Clifton StrengthsFinder?" https://www.leadershipvisionconsulting.com/what-is-the-clifton-strengthsfinder/, (accessed March 4, 2020).

Gallup. 2017. "State of the Global Workplace." https://www.gallup.com/workplace/238079/state-global-workplace-2017.aspx, (accessed March 4, 2020).

Gallup Organization. 2002. Workplace Poll. Internal Research Document.

Gilliard, M. n.d. "Bill Gates Leadership Style," *Leadership and Development. com.* https://leadership-and-development.com/bill-gates-leadership-style/, (accessed February 18, 2020).

Gladis, S. 2008. "Strengths Based Leadership." https://pdfs.semanticscholar.org/524a/4d676aa67cdeb9885cc55592a9fe9ddc0582.pdf, (accessed March 4, 2020).

Glock, J.W. 1955. "The Relative Value of Three Methods of Improving Reading--Tachistoscope, Films, and Determined Effort." PhD Thesis, University of Nebraska–Lincoln.

Glucksberg, S., and R.W. Weisberg. 1966. "Verbal Behavior and Problem Solving: Some Effects of Labeling in a Functional Fixedness Problem." *Journal of Experimental Psychology* 71, no. 5, p. 659.

Glucksberg, S. 1962. "The Influence of Strength of Drive on Functional Fixedness and Perceptual Recognition." *Journal of Experimental Psychology* 63, no. 1, p. 36.

Glucksberg, S. 1964. "Problem Solving: Response Competition and the Influence of Drive." *Psychological Reports* 15, no. 3, pp. 939–42.

Gneezy, U., and A. Rustichini. 2000. "A Fine Is a Price." *The Journal of Legal Studies* 29, no. 1, pp. 1–17.

Golubnichy, D. 2017. *Can You Be Happy for 100 Days in a Row?: The# 100HappyDays Challenge.* Artisan Books.

Govindji, R., and P.A. Linley. 2007. "Strengths Use, Self-Concordance and Well-being: Implications for Strengths Coaching and Coaching Psychologists." *International Coaching Psychology Review* 2, no. 2, 143–53.

Guest, D. 2002. "Human Resource Management, Corporate Performance and Employee Wellbeing: Building the Worker into HRM." *The Journal of Industrial Relations* 44, no. 3, pp. 335–58.

Harari, Y.N. 2014. *Sapiens: A Brief History of Humankind.* London, England: Random House.

Harms, P.D. 2017. "Gallup Strengths Finder." In *Encyclopedia of Personality and Individual Differences,* eds. V. Zeigler-Hill, T.K. Shackelford. New York, NY: Springer International Publishing, pp. 1–3.

Harter, J. 2017. "Dismal Employee Engagement Is a Sign of Global Mismanagement," *Gallup* Blog. www.gallup.com/workplace/231668/dismal-employee-engagement-sign-globalmismanagement.aspx, (accessed March 4, 2020).

Harzer, C., and W. Ruch. 2013. "The Application of Signature Character Strengths and Positive Experiences at Work." *Journal of Happiness Studies* 14, no. 3, pp. 965–83.

Harzer, C., and W. Ruch. 2014. "The Role of Character Strengths for Task Performance, Job Dedication, Interpersonal Facilitation, and Organizational Support." *Human Performance* 27, no. 3, pp. 183–205.

Harzer, C., and W. Ruch. 2012. "When the Job Is a Calling: The Role of Applying One's Signature Strengths at Work." *The Journal of Positive Psychology* 7, no. 5, pp. 362–71.

Haselton, M. 2018. *Hormonal: The Hidden Intelligence of Hormones--How They Drive Desire, Shape Relationships, Influence Our Choices, and Make Us Wiser.* London, England: Hachette.

Henseler, Jörg, Christian M. Ringle, and Marko Sarstedt. "A new criterion for assessing discriminant validity in variance-based structural equation modeling." *Journal of the academy of marketing science, 43,* no. 1 (2015): 115–135. doi:10.1007/s11747-014-0403-8.

Henson, R. 2011. "The Leadership of Steve Jobs," *Rutgers Business School.* http://business.rutgers.edu/business-insights/leadership-steve-jobs, (accessed March 4, 2020).

High5Test. 2019. "Statistical Reliability and Validity." https://high5test .com/methodology/reliability-validity/, (accessed March 4, 2020).

Hormone Health Network. 2018. "What Is Cortisol?" https://www .hormone.org/your-health-and-hormones/glands-and-hormones-a-to-z/hormones/cortisol, (accessed March 4, 2020).

Irlenbusch, B. 2009. "When Performance-related Pay Backfires," *London School of Economics.* http://lse.ac.uk/website-archive/newsAndMedia/news/ archives/2009/06/performancepay.aspx, (accessed June 9, 2018).

Isaacson, W. 2011. *Steve Jobs.* New York, NY: Simon & Schuster.

Isaacson, W. 2012. "The Real Leadership Lessons of Steve Jobs." *Harvard Business Review* 90, no. 4, pp. 92–102.

Judge, T.A., and C. Hurst. 2008. "How the Rich (and Happy) Get Richer (and Happier): Relationship of Core Self-evaluations to Trajectories in Attaining Work Success." *Journal of Applied Psychology* 93, no. 4, p. 849.

Kasser, T., and R.M. Ryan. 1993. "A Dark Side of the American Dream: Correlates of Financial Success as a Central Life Aspiration." *Journal of Personality and Social Psychology* 65, no. 2, p. 410.

Kerpen, D. 2014. "15 Quotes to Inspire Great Teamwork." https://www .inc.com/dave-kerpen/15-quotes-to-inspire-great-team-work.html, (accessed March 4, 2020).

Kirkland, R. 2009. *What Matters? Ten Questions That Will Shape Our Future.* McKinsey Management Institute, p. 80.

Kirschenbaum, D.S., A.M. Ordman, A.J. Tomarken, and R. Holtzbauer. 1982. "Effects of Differential Self-monitoring and Level of Mastery on Sports Performance: Brain Power Bowling." *Cognitive Therapy and Research* 6, no. 3, pp. 335–41.

Lazear, E. 2000. "The Peter Principle: Promotions and Declining Productivity," *Semantic Scholar*. https://pdfs.semanticscholar.org/2d12/ccf76e4cc072708 5078a637a6290e12aef49.pdf, (accessed June 9, 2018).

Lemyre, P.N., D.C. Treasure, and G.C. Roberts. 2006. "Influence of Variability in Motivation and Affect on Elite Athlete Burnout Susceptibility." *Journal of Sport and Exercise Psychology* 28, no. 1, pp. 32–48.

Lopez, Shane J., Tim Hodges, and Jim Harter. "The Clifton StrengthsFinder technical report: Development and validation." *Unpublished report* (2005).

Lopez, S.J., and C.R. Snyder, eds. 2003. *Positive Psychological Assessment: A Handbook of Models and Measures*. Washington, DC: American Psychological Association.

Luthans, F. 2011. *Organizational Behavior: An Evidence-based Approach*. 12th ed. New York, NY: McGraw-Hill/Irwin.

Luthans, F., C.M. Youssef, and B.J. Avolio. 2007. *Psychological Capital: Developing the Human Competitive Edge*. Oxford, England: Oxford University Press.

Martínez Sánchez, A., M. Pérez Pérez, P. de Luis Carnicer, and M. José Vela Jiménez. 2007. "Teleworking and Workplace Flexibility: A Study of Impact on Firm Performance." *Personnel Review* 36, no. 1, pp. 42–64.

Maslow, A.H. 1971. *The Farther Reaches of Human Nature*. New York, NY: Arkana/Penguin Books.

Matsudaira, K., A. Shimazu, T. Fujii, K. Kubota, T. Sawada, N. Kikuchi, and M. Takahashi. 2013. "Workaholism as a Risk Factor for Depressive Mood, Disabling Back Pain, and Sickness Absence." *PloS One* 8, no. 9, P. e75140.

Matson, T., and J. Robison. 2017. "The Rewarding Work of Turning Talents Into Strengths." https://news.gallup.com/businessjournal/202526/hard-work-turning-talents-strengths.aspx, (accessed March 4, 2020).

McAuley, M.T., R.A. Kenny, T.B.L. Kirkwood, D.J. Wilkinson, J.J.L. Jones, and V.M. Miller. 2009. "A Mathematical Model of Aging-related and Cortisol Induced Hippocampal Dysfunction." *BMC Neuroscience* 10, no., p. 26.

McCarville, B. 2020. "Snapshot: CliftonStrengths Theme Frequencies in Higher Education." https://www.strengthsquest.com/198197/snapshot-cliftonstrengths-theme-frequencies-higher-education.aspx#:~:

targetText=Because%20people%20are%20unique.,is%20one%20 in%2033.4%20million, (accessed March 4, 2020).

McClelland, D.C. 1951. "Measuring Motivation in Phantasy: The Achievement Motive." In *Groups, Leadership and Men; Research in Human Relations*, ed. H. Guetzkow. Oxford, England: Carnegie Press, pp. 191–205.

McCrae, R.R., J.E. Kurtz, S. Yamagata, and A. Terracciano. 2011. "Internal Consistency, Retest Reliability, and Their Implications for Personality Scale Validity." *Personality and Social Psychology Review* 15, no. 1, pp. 28–50.

McMillan, L.H.W., and M.P. O'Driscoll. 2004. "Workaholism and Health." *Journal of Organizational Change Management* 17, no. 5, pp. 509–19.

Minto, B. 2009. *The Pyramid Principle: Logic in Writing and Thinking*. Harlow, England: Pearson Education.

Morningstar, J.A. 2012. "Drives, Performance, Creativity and Introversion in the Workplace," *MPRA*. https://mpra.ub.uni-muenchen .de/62939/1/MPRA_ paper_62939.pdf, (accessed March 4, 2020).

Murray, H.A. 1938. *Explorations in Personality*. New York, NY: Oxford University Press.

Nakamura, J., and M. Csikszentmihalyi. 2009. "Flow Theory and Research." In *Handbook of Positive Psychology*, eds. C.R. Snyder, and S.J. Lopez. Oxford, MS: Oxford University Press, pp. 195–206.

Palacios, R.T., and I. Sugawara. 1982. "Hydrocortisone Abrogates Proliferation of T Cells in Autologous Mixed Lymphocyte Reaction by Rendering the Interleukin-2 Producer T Cells Unresponsive to Interleukin-1 and Unable to Synthesize the T-Cell Growth Factor." *Scandinavian Journal of Immunology* 15, no. 1, pp. 25–31.

Peterson, C. 2006. *A Primer in Positive Psychology*. New York, NY: Oxford University Press.

Pink, D. 2010. "The Autonomous Work Space." https://forbes.com/ 2010/04/29/best-buy-office-opinions-workspaces-daniel-pink, (accessed March 4, 2020).

Pink, D.H. 2011. *Drive: The Surprising Truth About What Motivates Us*. Canongate Books. Kindle Edition.

Pong, K. 2019. "Cliftonstrengths Theme Frequency All Countries 20 Million People." https://strengthsasia.com/cliftonstrengths-theme-frequency-all-countries-20-million-people-strengthsfinder/, (accessed March 4, 2020).

Proyer, R.T., F. Gander, S. Wellenzohn, and W. Ruch. 2013. "What Good Are Character Strengths Beyond Subjective Well-being? The Contribution of the Good Character on Self-reported Health-oriented Behavior, Physical Fitness, and the Subjective Health Status." *The Journal of Positive Psychology* 8, no. 3, pp. 222–32.

Gallup n. "Gallup Q12 Employee Engagement Survey". https://q12 .gallup.com/public/en-us/Features, (accessed March 4, 2020).

Rampton, J. 2016. "How Bill Gates Became a Leadership Legend," *Entrepreneur.com.* https://entrepreneur.com/article/250607, (accessed February 18, 2020).

Rath, T., B. Conchie. 2008. *Strengths Based Leadership: Great Leaders, Teams, and Why People Follow.* New Yok, NY: Simon and Schuster.

Rath, T. 2007. *StrengthsFinder 2.0.* New Yok, NY: Simon and Schuster.

Reilly, R. 2014. "Five Ways to Improve Employee Engagement Now." https:// www.gallup.com/workplace/231581/five-ways-improve-employee-engagement.aspx, (accessed March 4, 2020).

Reiss, S. 2004. "Multifaceted nature of intrinsic motivation: The theory of 16 basic desires." *Review of general psychology* 8, no. 3, 179–193.

Ridley, M. 2003. *Nature via Nurture: Genes, Experience, and What Makes Us Human.* New York, NY: HarperCollins.

Rose, T. 2016. *The End of Average: How to Succeed in a World That Values Sameness.* London, England: Penguin.

Ryan, R.M., and E.L. Deci. 2000. "Self-determination Theory and the Facilitation of Intrinsic Motivation, Social Development, and Well-being." *American Psychologist* 55, no. 1, p. 68.

Schreiner, L.A. 2006. "Technical Report on the Clifton StrengthsFinder with College Students." https://www.strengthsquest.com/192485/ technical-report-clifton-strengthsfinder-college-students.aspx, (accessed March 4, 2020).

Schulman, T., et al. 1998. "Dead Poets Society." Touchstone Home Video.

Seligman, M.E.P., R.M. Ernst, J. Gillham, K. Reivich, and M. Linkins. 2009. "Positive Education: Positive Psychology and Classroom Interventions." *Oxford Review of Education* 35, no. 3, pp. 293–311.

Seligman, M.E.P, T.A. Steen, N. Park, and C. Peterson. 2005. "Positive Psychology Progress: Empirical Validation of Interventions." *American Psychologist* 60, no. 5, p. 410.

Seligman, M.E.P. 2019. "Positive Psychology: A Personal History." https://www.annualreviews.org/doi/abs/10.1146/annurev-clinpsy-050718-095653, (accessed March 4, 2020).

Shuttleworth, M. 2019. "Test–Retest Reliability." https://explorable.com/test-retest-reliability, (accessed March 4, 2020).

Simmons, P.S., J.M. Miles, J.E. Gerich, and M.W. Haymond. 1984. "Increased Proteolysis. An Effect of Increases in Plasma Cortisol Within the Physiologic Range." *The Journal of Clinical Investigation* 73, no. 2, pp. 412–20.

Spence, J.T., and A.S. Robbins. 1992. "Workaholism: Definition, Measurement, and Preliminary Results." *Journal of Personality Assessment* 58, no. 1, pp. 160–78.

Sternberg, R.J., S.T. Fiske, and D.J. Foss, eds. 2016. *Scientists Making a Difference*. New York, NY: Cambridge University Press.

Sussman, S. 2012. "Workaholism: A Review." *Journal of Addiction Research & Therapy*, no. 1, p. 4120.

Suvorov, A. 2003. "Addiction to Rewards." Presentation delivered at the European Winter Meeting of the Econometric Society, October 25, 2013.

Taylor. M. 2019. "3 Reasons Why Motivation Alone Won't Make You Successful." https://everydaypower.com/motivation-alone-wont-make-you-successful/, (accessed March 4 2020).

ten Brummelhuis, L.L., C.L. ter Hoeven, A.B. Bakker, and B. Peper. 2011. "Breaking Through the Loss Cycle of Burnout: The Role of Motivation." *Journal of Occupational and Organizational Psychology* 84, no. 2, pp. 268–87.

Uk.coop. 2015. "The Cooperative Economy 2015" https://uk.coop/sites/default/files/uploads/attachments/co-op_economy_2015.pdf, (accessed February 18, 2020).

UPMC. 2016. "Chronic Stress Leads to Memory Loss as You Age." https://share.upmc.com/2016/06/stress-and-memory-loss/, (accessed March 4, 2020).

Van Wingerden, J., and J. Van der Stoep. 2018. "The Motivational Potential of Meaningful Work: Relationships with Strengths Use, Work Engagement, and Performance." *PloS One* 13, no. 6, p. e0197599.

van Woerkom, M., and M. de Bruijn. 2016. "Why Performance Appraisal Does Not Lead to Performance Improvement: Excellent Performance as a Function of Uniqueness Instead of Uniformity." *Industrial and Organizational Psychology* 9, no. 2, pp. 275–81.

van Woerkom, M., and M.C. Meyers. 2015. "My Strengths Count! Effects of a Strengths-Based Psychological Climate on Positive Affect and Job Performance." *Human Resource Management* 54, no. 1, pp. 81–103.

VIA. n.d. "The VIA Institute on Character". https://www.viacharacter .org/about, (accessed March 4, 2020).

Vitzthum, T. (2013). Deutsche Schüler wollen das Sitzenbleiben retten [German students want to save people from sitting down]. Retrieved from https://www.welt.de/politik/deutschland/article114159103/ Deutsche-Schueler-wollen-das-Sitzenbleiben-retten.html

Vitzthum V. Vol. 15:1-23. 2019. First published as a Review in Advance on December 10, 2018 https://doi.org/10.1146/annurev-clinpsy-050718-095653

Warrington, D. 2017. "FourFourTwo's 100 Greatest Footballers EVER: No.14, George Best." https://www.fourfourtwo.com/features/ fourfourtwos-100-greatest-footballers-ever-no14-george-best, (accessed February 28, 2020).

Wayman, E. 2012. "Mrs. Ples: A Hominid with an Identity Crisis." https://www.smithsonianmag.com/science-nature/mrs-ples-a-hominid-with-an-identity-crisis-59680909/, (accessed February 28, 2020).

White, M.A., and L.E. Waters. 2015. "A Case Study of 'The Good School': Examples of the Use of Peterson's Strengths-based Approach with Students." *The Journal of Positive Psychology* 10, no. 1, pp. 69–76.

Winne, P.H., and A.F. Hadwin. 2008. "The Weave of Motivation and Selfregulated Learning." In *Motivation and Self-regulated Learning: Theory, Research, and Applications*, eds. D. Schunk and B. Zimmerman. New York, NY: Routledge.

Wood, A.M., P.A. Linley, J. Maltby, T.B. Kashdan, and R. Hurling. 2011. "Using Personal and Psychological Strengths Leads to Increases in Well-being Over Time: A Longitudinal Study and the Development of the Strengths Use Questionnaire." *Personality and Individual Differences* 50, no. 1, pp. 15–19.

Zhu, D.J., and S. Zhang. 2014. "Research on Ecological Wellbeing Performance and Its Relationship with Economic Growth." *China Population, Resources and Environment* 24, no. 9, pp. 59–67.

About the Author

Matt L. Beadle is a British and German strengths mentor, management consultant, and facilitator who specializes in leadership development and strengths orientated leadership for young and new managers. After completing bachelor's and master's degrees at Greenwich and Birmingham City universities, respectively, Matt became a serial entrepreneur, setting up and running several companies before the sale of the last one in 2016. Since 2000, he has worked as a freelance management trainer and facilitator for Fortune 500 companies and global players across the world. He has trained or moderated over 20,000 executives of 40 different nationalities in over 20 countries and is one of the most renowned leadership experts working out of mainland Europe today.

Matt is married and lives together with his wife and their two children in Werther, Germany (where the famous sweets come from). He is a Chelsea fan, plays the guitar badly, loves making things out of wood, and his favorite candy bar is a Snickers. Matt is the author of two other books and is a regular speaker and presenter for business events, panel discussions, and TV shows.

www.mattbeadle.com

Index

OTHER TITLES IN THE HUMAN RESOURCE MANAGEMENT AND ORGANIZATIONAL BEHAVIOR COLLECTION

- *Transforming the Next Generation Leaders: Developing Future Leaders for a Disruptive, Digital-Driven Era of the Fourth Industrial Revolution (Industry 4.0)* by Sattar Bawany
- *Level-Up Leadership: Engaging Leaders for Success* by Michael J. Provitera
- *The Truth About Collaborating: Why People Fail and How to Succeed* by Dr. Gail Levitt
- *Uses and Risks of Business Chatbots: Guidelines for Purchasers in the Public and* Private Sectors by Tania Peitzker
- *Three Key Success Factors for Transforming Your Business: Mindset, Infrastructure, Capability* by Michael Hagemann
- *Hiring for Fit: A Key Leadership Skill* by Janet Webb
- *Successful Recruitment: How to Recruit the Right People For Your Business* by Stephen Amos
- *Uniquely Great Essentials for Winning Employers* by Lucy English
- *The Relevance of Humanities to the 21st Century Workplace* by Michael Edmondson
- *Untenable: A Leader's Guide to Addressing the Big Issues That Are Ignored, Falsely Explained, or Inappropriately Tolerated* by Gary Covert
- *Chief Kickboxing Officer Applying the Fight Mentality to Business Success* by Alfonso Asensio
- *Transforming the Next Generation Leaders: Developing Future Leaders for a Disruptive, Digital-Driven Era of the Fourth Industrial Revolution (Industry 4.0)* by Sattar Bawany
- *No Cape Required: Empowering Abundant Leadership* by Bob Hughes and Helen Caton Hughes
- *Cross-Cultural Leadership Studies* by Alan S. Gutterman
- *Comparative Management Studies* by Alan S. Gutterman
- *Breakthrough: Career Strategies for Women's Success* by Saundra Stroope
- *Women Leaders: The Power of Working Abroad* by Sapna Welsh and Caroline Kersten

Concise and Applied Business Books

The Collection listed above is one of 30 business subject collections that Business Expert Press has grown to make BEP a premiere publisher of print and digital books. Our concise and applied books are for...

- Professionals and Practitioners
- Faculty who adopt our books for courses
- Librarians who know that BEP's Digital Libraries are a unique way to offer students ebooks to download, not restricted with any digital rights management
- Executive Training Course Leaders
- Business Seminar Organizers

Business Expert Press books are for anyone who needs to dig deeper on business ideas, goals, and solutions to everyday problems. Whether one print book, one ebook, or buying a digital library of 110 ebooks, we remain the affordable and smart way to be business smart. For more information, please visit **www.businessexpertpress.com**, or contact **sales@businessexpertpress.com**.

www.ingramcontent.com/pod-product-compliance
Lightning Source LLC
Chambersburg PA
CBHW061320220326
41599CB00026B/4958